BOOK USE, BOOK THEORY: 1500–1700

Behaviovr.

ouing modesty

uing becomes

Complement.

wile Complement my best accomplishmen

Grace my guide

BOOK USE, BOOK THEORY: 1500–1700

Bradin Cormack and Carla Mazzio

UNIVERSITY OF CHICAGO LIBRARY

2005

2,000 copies of this catalog were published in conjunction with an exhibition held in the Special Collections Research Center, University of Chicago Library, March 8–June 17, 2005.

Support for this publication was provided by the University of Chicago Library Society.

ISBN: 0-943056-34-9

Design and typesetting by Joan Sommers Design

Copy-editing by Katherine Reilly

Photography by Ted Lacey, Patti Gibbons and Kerri Sancomb

Distributed by the University of Chicago Press
www.press.uchicago.edu

Printed in China by Asia Pacific Offset, Inc.

Bradin Cormack and Carla Mazzio are Assistant Professors of English at the University of Chicago

Images on the front and back covers are from catalog items 3, 8, 10 and 22.

Frontispiece and half-title are details from Richard Brathwaite, *The English Gentlewoman* (London: by B. Alsop and T. Fawcet, 1631). Not in catalog.

Capitalization and forms of letters i, j, u, v have been retained as they appear in the original.

CONTENTS

PREFACE

OF ALL THE WAYS TO USE BOOKS, exhibiting them may be the oddest. Works of art such as paintings and sculpture are created to be viewed, and museums place them on display to provide access to them. Museum-goers can study and enjoy the item (out of its original context, for example a church or home) and learn something about the environment within and for which it was created. Books are produced for use by individuals; and libraries facilitate their discovery by collecting, organizing and describing books known or likely to be useful to potential readers. In a library, accessibility is defined by the ease with which researchers can identify and locate needed materials, not by how many or which ones are visible. When not in use, books sit on shelves awaiting their readers, and miles of shelving merely suggest the riches they hold. When selected for an exhibition, a book becomes inaccessible to the individual who may wish to consult it (although it can be removed on a temporary basis); installed in a locked case behind glass, it is not usable by anyone. Only one page or double-spread opening of a book can be displayed, at least in its original form, and books are not constructed physically to be held open at the same page for long periods of time. A three-dimensional, interactive tool for learning or pleasure is thus transformed into a piece of sculpture to be observed at a distance.

What then, is the use of book exhibitions? Why would a library remove a group of books from circulation to place them on display? Exhibitions of books, manuscripts and archival materials certainly promote knowledge of available resources and stimulate further investigation of a particular collection or subject. And they are often the occasion for, and product of, substantial research that is then shared with a larger audience. Book exhibitions are all about creating context—they place individual works into a bibliographical, biographical or historical framework—and construct a narrative in which physical books serve as exemplars and evidence.

Library exhibitions also foster new ways of thinking about—and using—books. In fact, displacing a book from its natural home forces us to see it differently. Book exhibitions direct our attention to the physical object: the text it contains may be pertinent to the theme of the show, but since we cannot read it we are free to consider other aspects of what is on view. We inspect the title page or other opening, read and learn from the information provided; the books themselves are examples that make the "case" of the show. We look at them rather than read them, and in the process observe physical features and see distinctions that prompt reflection.

Book Use, Book Theory: 1500–1700, published in conjunction with an exhibition of the same title, takes this concept much further. Bradin Cormack and Carla Mazzio examine the diverse uses of early modern books, as imagined by authors and implemented by readers, and the physical characteristics and textual features that support these applications. In the period between 1500 and 1700, printed books played an important role in shaping language use, ways of knowing, and professional practice in fields such as law and medicine. As *Book Use, Book Theory* illustrates, writers and printers exploited physical features such as size and page layout, apparatus such as indexes or titles, as well as graphic material. Readers added their own marks—in bindings and marginalia—to make the book a more useful reflection of their purpose. *Book Use, Book Theory* makes an important contribution to book history by exploring how book use evolved, and how early writers reflected on that process, in the two centuries following the invention of printing.

I am delighted that Professors Cormack and Mazzio grounded their scholarship in an exhibition for the Special Collections Research Center. Over the course of their extensive research, Professors Cormack and Mazzio examined a large number of books from across the entire range of the collection, and uncovered new ways of looking at, reading and using them. Use of this nature involves a great many staff members to page, circulate, track and reshelve materials. I extend sincere thanks to Barbara Gilbert, Debra Levine, Jay Satterfield, Susan Summerfield, Anne Taylor and numerous other staff and student assistants in Special Collections for their essential contributions to this project. Catherine Uecker, Rare Books Coordinator, edited the bibliographic entries.

The research process also became a reflection on using books in an exhibition. Professors Cormack and Mazzio were intensely engaged in exploring the conceptual implications of design and production. Kerri Sancomb, Exhibition Specialist, proposed imaginative and effective solutions to the physical realities of the exhibition space. As a result of these varied perspectives, *Book Use, Book Theory* serves as a model for how producing, as well as viewing, library exhibitions can contribute to learning about and through books.

— ALICE SCHREYER
Director
Special Collections Research Center

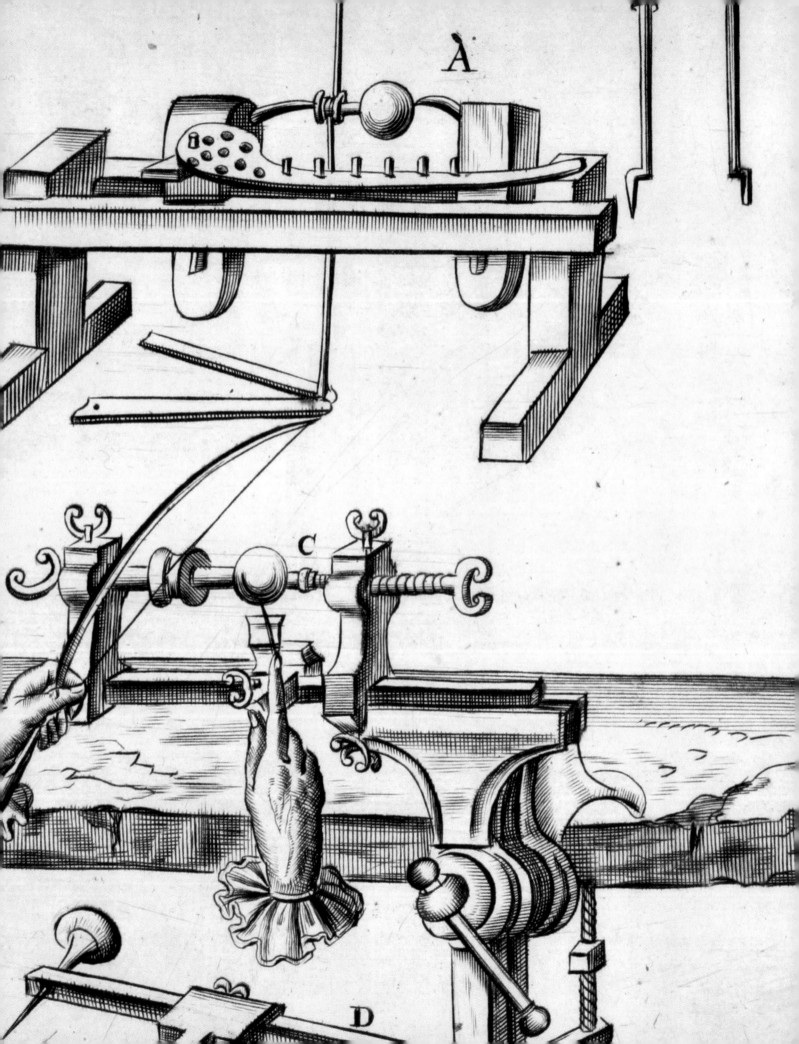

ACKNOWLEDGMENTS

A PRODUCT OF MANY HANDS, this book was continually energized by our colleagues, students and friends. We are particularly grateful for the generosity of David Bevington, Paul Gehl, William Ingram, Elizabeth Ingram, Janice Knight, Jeffrey Masten, Janel Mueller, Michael Murrin, Stephen Orgel, Joshua Phillips, Joshua Scodel, Eric Slauter, Peter Stallybrass and Richard Strier. Book use always implies a series of relations between objects and persons and between individuals and collectives. For enabling us to actually use the books we explore here, we also thank all the staff members at the University of Chicago Library's Special Collections Research Center.

Book Use, Book Theory is based on an exhibition that we curated for the Special Collections Research Center in 2005, and we are very grateful to Kerri Sancomb for her work on the images and exhibition design. In particular, we want to thank the Center's director, Alice Schreyer, for her support, from encouraging our initial ideas for the exhibition to facilitating the publication of this book. Alice has proved a magnificent colleague and collaborator—without her, this book would not have been possible.

This is a book about use that we hope will be used, reused, and even (in terms of this book) misused. For inspiring us to use books in new ways, and to create a work about early modern book use and book theory, we would also like to thank our students. Using primary resources in Special Collections, as well as *Early English Books Online* and facsimile reprints, our students continuously redefine early book use and its relevance for reading as a form of social, theoretical and imaginative engagement.

— BRADIN CORMACK AND CARLA MAZZIO

DETAIL, CAT. 42

Use, Misuse and the Making of Book Theory: 1500–1700

From Whitney, *Choice of Emblemes*

THE CONCEPT OF BOOK USE is integral to the history of reading in early modern Europe and to the theory of the book itself. In his 1586 *Choice of Emblemes*, Geffrey Whitney includes a striking emblem that distinguishes between using books and merely reading them.[1] The motto, "*Usus libri, non lectio prudentes facit*" ("Using a book, not reading it, makes us wise"), is printed above an illustration of two figures, one at a lectern leaning over a large folio volume, his hand touching the book's right-hand page, the other standing slightly apart from the scene of reading. The accompanying poem expands on the motto by reflecting on the benefits of use, and on the difference between what it means to "peruse" and "use" a book:

> The volumes great, who so doth still peruse,
> And dailie turnes, and gazeth on the same,
> If that the fruicte thereof, he do not vse,

He reapes but toile, and never gaineth fame:
> Firste reade, then marke, then practise that is good,
> For without vse, we drinke but LETHE flood.

Of practise longe, experience doth proceede;
And wisedome then, doth euermore ensue:
Then printe in minde, what wee in printe do reade,
Els loose wee time, and bookes in vaine do vewe:
> Wee maie not haste, our talent to bestowe,
> Nor hide it vp, whereby no good shall growe.

At first glance, Whitney's account of reading books and using books seems to follow the familiar distinction between theoretical knowledge and practical knowledge: reading is valuable only if its "fruits" are put to use. This ideal resonates with the civic humanist emphasis on the importance of doing, rather than simply knowing, of using book knowledge to produce "a responsible, moral and active member of the civic community."[2]

But Whitney's distinction is more radical, since without use his reader is left without any knowledge at all and only with "toile." Use, in other words, is positioned as the foundation of practice and experience, but also, more surprisingly, of memory and knowledge itself. Although reading for Whitney means rereading, a laborious process in which one "dailie turnes, and gazeth on the same," reading by itself is so far from leading to wisdom as to be ineffectual even for remembering the words on the page: "For without vse, we drinke but LETHE flood." The typographic amplification of Lethe, the mythic river of forgetfulness, at once commands the reader's attention and highlights the danger of oblivion that follows from merely gazing on words. In contrast, book use involves not just the practical application of printed words in the world but also their internalization as "printe" in "minde." In this vividly material process, remembering is a mental copying aligned with mechanical reproduction, so that reading-as-use essentially reprints the book, but this time in a form useful to a single individual.

Use simultaneously relocates the book to the intimate, private space of an individual's mind and makes an otherwise hidden knowledge public, thereby embedding the reader in the social realm. It is therefore significant that Whitney's illustration of book use features not a solitary reader but two figures, and that both are standing rather than sitting, a posture that identifies the scene of reading with action. Together, the figures can be seen to represent the ideal textual community that the poem emphasizes in its shift from a reading "he" to a using "we." Indeed, rather than seeing the figures as personifications, respectively, of reading and use, theory and practice, we can instead understand them as representing the dual nature of book use emphasized by Whitney: the figure on the left stands ready to put knowledge to use, while his double at the lectern, who engages the book with eye and hand, transforms reading itself into a kind of doing or acting. In the same way, Whitney's poem splits book use into two kinds of practice, one textual and one worldly, positioning them both against mere reading: "Firste reade, then marke, then practise that is good."

According to this dictum, to use a book is to experience it in time. In fact, the three-part engagement with the book that Whitney recommends mirrors the tripartite temporality of prudence, which the emblem's motto identifies as the virtue to be gained by using books well.[3] Prudence, as a form of practical wisdom, was traditionally understood to look to past, present and future, by combining memory, intelligence and foresight. Most simply, the trajectory in Whitney of reading, marking and practicing relates to prudence because it bridges the book's past, the reading present and a future practice beyond the book. Understood in terms of prudence, the three stages of book use become inextricably linked and philosophically charged. First, we can note that Whitney recuperates reading by placing it *in time*: in contrast to a reading that, unmoored from use, results in the loss of memory, active engagement secures memory because it brings words from the past into the present and so allows the reader not to "loose . . . time." Marking a book, similarly, is both a memory technique (underscoring material on the page helps to impress it in the mind) and a material practice that registers reading as always belonging to the present, the moment of putting pen to printed page.[4] Equally, of course, marking something as memorable is a way for a reader to note something useful for the future, in a domain of practice beyond the book.[5]

The poem thus unfolds the philosophical stakes of book use: the virtue of a book, its force for "good," depends on the reader's awareness that books, far from being historically fixed, are part of an ongoing historical process in which readers are central agents. Readers make book knowledge valuable when they identify it as memorable, as something *worth* remembering. Whitney thus places the reader at the center of a cultural process of book use that secures the continuity of knowledge. His reformed reader is a cultural hero. It is telling, then, that the emblem offers "fame" as the reward for using books well. Certainly, this fame arises from the user's translating books into action, words into deeds. But fame in this period was also quintessentially textual, the traditional reward promised the poet or author, the creator of the text.[6] Reconfiguring textual authority in light of use, Whitney instead offers fame to the book's consumer, the reader whose use makes the book memorable by making it his or her own and so producing it anew.

Because Whitney's emblem empties both reading and writing of their traditional authority in order to redefine their value in relationship to use, it is a helpful starting point for this study, which historicizes books as objects of use. The idea of book *use* helps make visible the set of material, social and institutional relations in which books are embedded and also help constitute. In the early modern period with which we are concerned, printed books were primarily understood as instrumental, directing their readers and users, within particular fields of practice or knowledge, toward some more or less practical end. Where books such as romances were criticized, it was nearly always in terms of their lack of practical utility. "Useful" books taught people to do things, to acquire skills and move up in the world, to be a particular kind of person or a better person. Others transmitted knowledge central to the construction of disciplinary fields and professional prestige. And of course books of all kinds, including romances, taught people how to think or think in new ways. In the early years of print, this latter goal often involved teaching readers how to engage with the book itself as a set of possibly unfamiliar forms. Indeed, if books were instrumental, they were very explicitly also instruments, intricate tools that needed to be used in order to become useful.

Book Use, Book Theory: 1500–1700 focuses on the relationship between a book's social functions and the textual and technical aspects that made the material book and its contents usable and knowable. Drawing on professional texts in the disciplines of law and medicine, on literary, religious and scientific texts, and on how-to manuals for practices such as cooking, measuring, praying and traveling, we explore how early books enabled thinking by inviting a wide range of uses, by asking readers to move within them in particular ways, to write in them, manipulate them, apply them in worlds beyond the book. If genres such as the how-to book encouraged forms of thinking inseparable from practice, paper technologies such as foldouts and volvelles (movable wheels useful for various calculations) made the page itself into a site of scientific practice. Understanding the early book as a practical tool makes it possible, that is, to see its many material forms in terms of the knowledge systems that both shaped and were shaped by them.

To use a book is to engage with it as a set of forms and as a condition of thought; in this sense, the history of book use and the history of theoretical speculation are entwined. Indeed, when authors or printers deployed textual forms to make books more navigable or useful, they often reflected upon those technologies to emphasize the book's relation to specific fields of knowledge and specific forms of thinking. Textual theory, this catalog argues, emerged through such reflections on the potential for books to be useful, usable and used.

MATERIAL EFFECTS: BOOK AND BODY

The early modern book could be used in very simple ways: as paperweight, a press for flowers, or a secret or convenient container; the owner of one book printed in 1503 hollowed out a space in the binding for holding spectacles.[7] And books functioned then as now as objects of exchange whose value as such did not necessarily depend on their content, but rather on their status precisely as prize or gift or memento. Such uses magnify the book's materiality. That said, the book's physical dimensions were equally central to those forms of use in which content mattered a great deal. Historians of the book have long given priority to the fact that books are objects, and that their material forms are integral to their meaning and to the reading practices that help constitute that meaning. In contrast to a potentially abstract or disembodied notion of reading, then, using a book always suggests a physical engagement with it: as a volume to be held or leaned over, as paper to write on, or indeed as a paper technology for producing meaning. Thinking through books means thinking in and around them.

It is, of course, quite possible to read without paying attention to the artifactual nature of the book, and even to imagine the reading process as antithetical to the material. In his 1588 account of his meeting with the American Algonquians, Thomas Hariot in fact encourages, as against a sensuous and material use of the book, an abstracted form of reading that leaves the book (and the body) behind:

> Manie times and in euery towne where I came . . . I made declaration of the contentes of the Bible; that therein was set foorth the true and onelie GOD, and his mightie woorkes, that therein was contayned the true doctrine of saluation through Christ, with manie particularities of Miracles and chiefe poyntes of religion, as I was able then to vtter, and thought fitte for the time. And although I told them the booke materially & of itself was not of anie such vertue, as I thought they did conceiue, but onely the doctrine therein contained; yet would many be glad to touch it, to embrace it, to kisse it, to hold it to their brests and heades, and stroke ouer all their bodie with it; to shewe their hungrie desire of that knowledge which was spoken of.[8]

Hariot distinguishes here between the physical book, "the booke materially & of itself," and the contents of the book, aligning these with inappropriate and appropriate forms of use. He describes the indigenous Americans in terms of the intra-European religious conflict between Protestant and Catholic;[9] here Hariot's Protestantism draws him away from Catholic idolatry and toward Protestant scripturalism, which is to say, away from the book as object and toward the book as a dematerialized medium. In this respect, it is striking that the name Hariot gives to the textual content he values is the conspicuously abstracted "doctrine," as opposed to a term like "the Word," which might have hinted at a residual materiality.[10]

And yet Hariot's own account also unsettles any clear separation of the book's subject from its object form. Hariot's insistence that God and the doctrine of salvation are "set forth" "therein" implies material form and dimension; the force of his evangelism depends on the book as a prop and a locus of his authority, as one instance of the "advanced technology" through which, in Stephen Greenblatt's formulation, colonial power made its "impression. . . upon a 'backward' people."[11] For their part, the Algonquians' extraordinary emphasis on the book as a love object, something to be touched, embraced, kissed, held and stroked, expresses a relationship precisely to the book's subject matter, namely "that knowledge which was spoken of." If Hariot's disavowal of the book as object falls short of fully separating matter and meaning, this is partly because the Algonquian response he records is on a continuum not only with Catholic practice but also with the Protestant insistence on a personal relationship to the Bible. In Mary Rowlandson's 1682 account of her captivity, this is a materially imagined relationship: turning to her Bible for both spiritual and physical comfort, she calls it "my guid by day, and my Pillow by night."[12] For Rowlandson, as for the Algonquians, the book is metonymic for its own contents, so that using it by touching it (or being touched by it) can even constitute a kind of reading.

The book emerges here as a material object, subject to use. Like Whitney's emblem, Hariot's narrative is useful to book history because it suggests the limits of idealizing the text. It also unsettles the logic through which an investment in the material book is understood as mere disavowal of content, easily equated with idolatry or fetishism. As Ann Rosalind Jones and Peter Stallybrass point out in relation to the fetish, "What was demonized in the concept of the fetish was the possibility that history, memory, and desire might be materialized in objects that are touched and loved and worn."[13] Books too are such objects. In his 1522 colloquy "The Godly Feast," the humanist

Erasmus has his character Eusebius mark the value of classical texts by acknowledging them precisely as objects to be touched:

> Sacred Scripture is of course the basic authority in everything; yet I sometimes run across ancient sayings or pagan writings—even the poets'—so purely and reverently and admirably expressed that I can't help believing their authors' hearts were moved by some divine power . . . . Among friends, I confess my love: I can't read Cicero's *On Old Age, On Friendship,* his *Offices,* his *Tusculan Disputations* without sometimes kissing the book.[14]

As with Rowlandson, we are very close here to the "book practices" that Hariot attempts to banish.

The interactions between body and book in Hariot, Rowlandson and Erasmus all express an affective relation to content. They thus remind us just how intimate the relation is between engaging a book physically and engaging it cognitively. Although the touch required for reading may not itself be sensuous or affective, it is always integral to the ways in which a reader makes a book his or her own. Anyone familiar with old books knows the look and feel of a well-thumbed page. In a more complex sense, Peter Stallybrass has noted the importance of actual fingers for the history of biblical interpretation, since the index finger, used as a bookmark, was itself a technology for discontinuous reading, used by readers to generate meaning by moving between passages in different parts of the Bible. That kind of discontinuous reading was formalized through a series of navigational tools for the reader, including the division of chapter into verse (a system first introduced in the early sixteenth century), interpretive glosses and the indexes and concordances that were, as Stallybrass points out, often bound with scripture into a composite volume.[15]

NAVIGATING BOOKS: FORMAT AND USE

Far from being secondary to content, the physical forms of the book generate content by making it available for particular kinds of use. A book's format shapes the body's interaction with it—is it small enough to fit in a pocket or light enough to be carried; is there room in its margins for a hand to write in; does pagination or indexing inform the hand's movement from page to page; does the page require the reader to unfold or manipulate the paper; does the layout direct the eye in particular ways in order to facilitate the processing of information? As the material book informs use it shapes meaning. On the one hand, readers generate meaning by using books with their hands and eyes, in their own particular ways. On the other, the concept of book use as an ideal helped producers of books refine the print technologies that could at once attract readers and guide them in the production of meaning. When writers and printers reflected on the ways in which a particular book was useful, they were in effect inventing book theory, by theorizing this or that book in terms of the *efficacy* of its material features.

The significance of a book's format for its meaning and use value is vividly exemplified in the relationship between two medical books printed by William Jaggard: Helkiah Crooke's 1615 *Mikrokosmographia: A Description of the Body of Man* (cat. 70) and Alexander Read's 1616 *Somatographia Anthropine: Or A Description of the Body of Man*. Read's book reproduces in tabular form information in Crooke, digesting the earlier book's complex narratives into simple lists (as compared with Crooke's one thousand folio pages, Read's book takes up only three hundred quarto pages). Most strikingly, Read reconfigures the page layout so as to clearly separate word from image: whereas Crooke's volume intersperses text and illustrations on the same page, Read's places illustration and text on facing pages, the anatomical figures on the left and the anatomical index on the right. Read's explicit debt to Crooke compels him to defend his book in the preface, where he imagines that "some nice Criticke" will find the book "altogether unnecessarie, both by reason of the matter and of the Language," given that "M. Doctor *Crooke*" has already expressed the contents so well in English that no "monument of this subiect can be expected, which wil be more excellent."[16] What makes Read's book valuable, however, is precisely its more useful format. Quite the opposite of a monument, it is a manual, a book to be used as it is held. In the first place, Read points out, Crooke's larger book is "not portable"; more interestingly, Crooke's mixing of text and image on single pages works to "distract the minde, and defraud the store-house of memory." In contrast, Read continues, his own "small volume":

> presenting all the partes of the body of man by continuation to the eie, impresseth the Figures firmly in the mind, and being portable may be carried without trouble, to the places appointed for dissection: where the collation of the Figures, with the Descriptions, cannot but affoord great contentment to the mind. The Printer therefore of the former great volume, hath published this small Manuell, hoping it will prooue profitable and delightfull to such as are not able to buy, or haue no time to peruse the other.[17]

The passage at once advertises and theorizes the book. As one among many marketing strategies, for example, size allows the book literally to enter the scene of professional practice. But Read further claims that his book's size and layout facilitate the process of knowledge acquisition itself, since the reorganization of an otherwise distracting combination of text and image improves the reader's concentration.[18] In Read's terms, the book's contents are brought into alignment with the scale and organization of the human "store-house of memory."

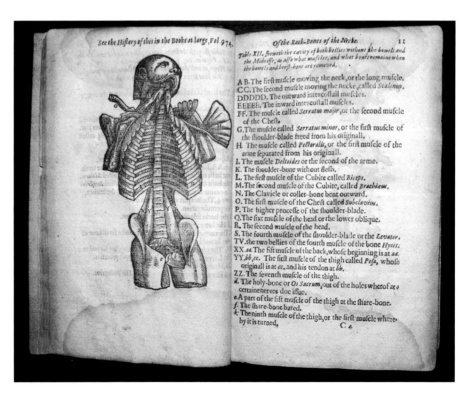

Alexander Read, *Somatographia Anthropine* (1616, from 1634 ed.)

This process of internalization or intellectual "contentment," then, is a second way in which the book becomes portable—in the individual practitioner's mind. Read's reflection on the format of his book as a useful vehicle for thought and practice constitutes a theory both of his book and of the book.

Despite Read's emphasis on the autonomy of his book, its format in fact also works to unsettle that autonomy, as for example in its systematic crossreferencing of Crooke's volume. So it is interesting that the figure illustrated here, both anatomical subject and a potential reader of the index to his body, directs his gaze in two places at once. Even as he seems, in stretching his neck, to look at Read's own subject heading, "Of the Rack-bones of the Neck," his eye also falls on the page number in Crooke's volume to which the reader is directed: "See the History of this in the Booke at large, Fol. 974." If Read theorizes his book as a substitute for Crooke's, the system of cross-referencing also points to the interdependence of the books and the situations of use they enable. The cross-referencing in effect transforms Read's practical book into an index and advertisement for Crooke's more elaborate volume.

Read's book is typical in promoting its utility in terms of specific textual forms, and in so doing imagining the social significance of its use. Crooke himself makes a similar point in his medical textbook, both when he advertises anatomy as the most useful "among all the parts of our Art," and when he distinguishes his book from his Latin sources, precisely by foregrounding how he has made his book more usable: "The Method I haue altered throughout, transported the Tables as seemed best vnto me, reuised and made choise of the quotations . . . and interposed them in their owne places. I also added Praefaces to euery booke conteining the argument and purport thereof."[19] Even Crooke's use of English can be thought of as a textual strategy: writing in Latin, he says, would have been easier for him, but "it had bin most ydle, my purpose being to better them who do not so wel vnderstand that language."[20] English, in other words, makes his anatomical compendium useful to his country and his profession. What deserves emphasis here is how both Crooke and Read amplify the utility of their textual forms in order to advance the theoretical significance of those forms for both textual and professional practice. In the early modern period, when the professions were still in formation, such claims to utility had a particular theoretical import since the category of usefulness was so important for defining the contours of the developing professions.[21]

USE AND ITS DISCONTENTS: ABRIDGMENT, INDEX, ILLUSTRATION

Although a book's value was in part defined by its ability to make knowledge accessible and usable, the very technologies that accomplished this could be seen, in other terms, to oversimplify the learning process and so undermine the book's use-value. Read imagines his small book as a useful substitute for Crooke, available, as he says, to those who have neither the money to buy nor the "time to peruse the other." As a substitute unmoored from its source, however, his abridgment could be more an impediment than an aid to learning. Indeed, early print genres such as the abridgment, epitome or printed commonplace book, whose purpose was to facilitate a reader's access to information, were in general a site of intense concern for those who felt they compromised the integrity of knowledge or professional practice. In his 1570 *Scholemaster*, the humanist Roger Ascham complained in these terms about printed commonplace books, which offered the reader predigested textual material organized under set categories and thus could substitute for the interpretive reading process itself. Although such books are useful, he says, for bringing thoughts into order and thereby helping a student "not [to] wander in studie," they become dangerous when treated as the foundation of knowledge:

> But to dwell in *Epitomes* and bookes of common places, and not to binde himselfe dailie by orderlie studie, to reade with all diligence . . . maketh so many seeming . . . ministers as we haue.[22]

For Ascham, the selection or synopsis is valuable, then, as a model for the reader's own active textual engagement. Writing in 1604 about the law, Sir Edward Coke similarly makes the reader's active engagement with an unwieldy and difficult text paramount. Abridgments for Coke threaten the acquisition of real knowledge if used as anything more than a memory aid:

> This I know, that abridgements in many professions haue greatly profited the Authors themselues; but as they are vsed haue brought no small preiudice to others: For the aduised and orderly reading ouer of the Bookes at large . . . I absolutely determine to be the right way to enduring and perfect knowledge, and to vse abridgements as tables, and to trust onely to the Bookes at large . . . . And certaine it is that the tumultuarie reading of Abridgements, doth cause a confused iudgement, and a broken and troubled kind of deliuerie or vtterance.[23]

If overused, the very tool intended to organize difficult material becomes an obstacle to methodical thinking. Notable here is how the abridgment transforms reading itself from an "aduised and orderly" practice into a "tumultuarie" or undisciplined one that compromises professional practice and performance. In accounts like Coke's or Ascham's, textual shortcuts or cribs are dangerous, because they can only simulate the internal cognitive processes toward which writing and reading should be oriented. In Francis Bacon's formulation, "one Man's Notes will little profit another, because one man's Conceit doth so much differ from another's."[24]

Epitomes and abridgments came into being as a response to the phenomenon of print itself. Emphasizing the destabilizing effects of the early modern press, Ann Blair has cataloged how authors, printers and readers responded to a disorienting "information overload" and unwieldy "over-abundance of books" by producing reference works like dictionaries and concordances and by refining navigational tools within the book such as the index, preface or table of contents.[25] As Neil Rhodes and Jonathan Sawday note, even the spatial arrangement of the printed page, "with its system of sections and subsections, footnotes, marginal notes and paragraph divisions," constituted an early information technology: "different typefaces might denote hierarchies of information; graphics and illustrations, sometimes (in the case of medical works) deploying the new device of a keying mechanism to relate word and image, complemented what was to be found in the text."[26]

All such print strategies promote the book's utility, in the sense sometimes of actually making the book easier to use and, sometimes, in the sense only of *advertising* the book's utility. A feature such as the index, for example, promises to make a work navigable by framing it, by identifying its categories, by digesting and ordering its details. Thus Stephen Orgel points out that for encyclopedic texts like Piero Valeriano's 1556 *Hieroglyphica* or Philemon Holland's 1601 translation of Pliny's natural history, the "inclusion of a very elaborate and genuinely usable index" was central both to the value of the books and, in the case of Holland, to its all-important "claim to compendiousness." That said, as Orgel also notes, early modern indexes can be conspicuously erratic, as for example the seven-page index that accompanied the second edition of Robert Burton's *Anatomy of Melancholy* and all early editions thereafter: "characteristic entries under *A* include 'All are melancholy' and 'All beautiful parts attractive in love'; under *B*, 'Best site of an house' and 'Black eyes best.' Though bugloss wine is said in the text to be effective in curing leprosy, neither bugloss nor leprosy is indexed."[27]

At issue here is the nature of the index as a technology of selection. Even when an index seems to be neutral, by its nature it is interpretive since it guides cognition by emphasizing certain categories and eliding others and indeed by implicitly defining what constitutes a category. So it is telling that, although Burton's index is conspicuously incomplete, its entries can be read, too, as excessively scrupulous, as though engendered by a fantasy of comprehensiveness, according to which "all" is no less significant than "melancholy," nor the adjectives "black" and "best" less so than "eyes." This leveling out may be in part a function of alphabetization, a principle of indexical arrangement that became the norm only in this period. In contrast to indexes that order material according to preordained and "natural" schemes, the alphabetic index is arbitrary and as such neither determines a hierarchy of meaning nor provides conceptual criteria for its own subject headings. The effect of this kind of index in disrupting categorical thinking is nowhere more apparent in Burton's index than under *H* and *W*, where the alphabet has allowed the indexer to include "how often tis fit to eat in a day"; "how men fall in loue";

"What physicke fit in loue mel[ancholy]; "Who are most apt to be iealous"; "Why fooles beget wise children, wisemen fooles."[28] These entries render the apparently dominant category (love, fools, jealousy) contingent. At the same time, they are strikingly continuous with the function and idea of the index, since they isolate as categories the words (or topics) that underwrite the idea of orientation itself: how, who, what, why. The irregularities of Burton's index can, certainly, be attributed to the fact that indexical technology was not yet standard-ized. But it is important to stress also how well, in fact, this index "points to" its book, by mirroring the priority given to the particular by Burton. Treating melancholy, a topic that defies categorization, and for that reason deploying infinite particulars and digressions and intermingling genres, Burton's book exults in its own irreducible particularities and contingencies. Exactly by upsetting what might constitute a relevant particular, the index underlines how in Burton's text as a whole, as Richard Strier puts it, "particulars matter" and ground thought.[29]

Burton's index is suggestive for book history in a number of ways: it reminds us that technologies of navigation were not always useful and indeed that the *illusion* of navigability alone might make the book commercially attractive. More interestingly, it is precisely the apparent failure of Burton's index to deliver, to be useful, that makes it visible as an essential part of the process of producing meaning. A techno-logy that works, that orients cognition in a way that proves consis-tently useful, comes of course to look familiar or natural and so not like a technology at all.[30] Indeed, the most significant dimension of Burton's index is the underlying idea that a book like his, this "rhap-sody of rags gathered from several dunghills, excrements of authors, toys and fopperies confusedly tumbled out," could be effectively indexed at all. We would not today think naturally of indexing a novel, unless of course it was a postmodern one; and the point of that index would be precisely to reflect on the index as a medium-specific technology for generating meaning.

Thomas Corns, in fact, points to an innovative indexical feature in an early book that is strikingly self-reflexive in confronting the limits of the print medium. The index he has in mind is the illustrated title page to Thomas Coryate's 1611 *Coryats Crudities*, a page, he says, that helps constitute the book as an early version of hypertext. Using letters of the alphabet to direct the reader from its various illustrated scenes to one of thirteen explanatory epigrams and then into Coryate's narrative itself, the indexical page effectively maps out the book. Even as it points the reader forward, however, it points to the "limitations of flat texts and the serial transmission of information, offering instead other avenues of access, more spatial ways of thinking and of reading, and of relating one level of discourse to other levels."[31]

Coryate's page takes to an extreme the potential for illustrations more generally to reflect upon textual content, often by disrupting a purely sequential engagement with the book. Like an index at a book's beginning or end, and like prefaces that framed authorized texts (frequently by hyperbolizing their use value), pictorial illustrations stand both outside the text and in conspicuous relation to it. Illustrations were useful in a number of ways. In scientific books like William Cowper's *Anatomy of Humane Bodies* (cat. 8) or Robert Hooke's *Micrographia* (cat. 10), as in manuals for craftsmen like Albrecht Dürer's *Art of Measurement* (cat. 1), pictures often provided crucial visual data that text alone could not represent. By depicting prior or idealized scenes of practice (at the microscope, for example, or the dissecting table), such images could function, furthermore, as a substitute for practice: the reader's movement back and forth between picture and text as mutually informing technologies of representation remade scientific practice as textual practice. A book like Johan Remmelin's multilayered flap anatomy (cat. 62) makes this relationship unusually explicit, since it requires the reader not only to relate the textual index of body parts to the anatomical diagram on the opposite page, but also to unfold the body, paper layer by paper layer, in a process of discovery that mimics dissection. The practical utility of anatomical illustration is differently theorized in a plate from William Cowper's *Anatomy*, whose massive pages are large enough to allow for actual-scale representation of particular body parts. The plate, shown here and on page 47, represents a dissected arm emerging from a folio volume much like Cowper's own. The image self-consciously conflates book use and anatomical dissection, by

CAT. 8

merging paper and body, the materials that subtend the practices. The image is an illustration about illustration. It is the book looking back at itself, theorizing itself from the perspective of practices both inside and outside the book. It is no surprise that the image plays too on the notion of the index, with the second finger of the dead hand pointing both to the "table" for dissection and to the pages of the book that lie beneath its touch.

Like the other technologies we have been exploring, however, the function of pictorial illustrations was not always transparent. Reflecting on early illustrations that seem "illogical, inappropriate, or simply wrong," Stephen Orgel points out that when images fail to convey useful information, they can often be seen to be about the book itself, "part of the rhetoric of the book" as a particular kind of material object. The point of the abundantly and even excessively illustrated *Nuremberg Chronicle*, with the same woodblocks used to represent different cities and personages was, he suggests, to show "that typography can produce books that are as lavishly illustrated as the most beautiful manuscripts."[32] Rather than supplementing subject matter, in other words, such images illustrate the book's status as a technology and aesthetic. That said, apparently dysfunctional images sometimes did have a profound relation to subject matter. The woodcut illustrations that accompany the narratives of English Protestant martyrdom in John Foxe's *Acts and Monuments* (cat. 32) are glossed with the name of the martyr and the date and place of death; they thus seem to mirror the book's insistent identification and valorization of the particular person and life. It thus seems disconcerting that several of the woodcuts are used multiple times, and that they come as generic images to eclipse the particularity they seem to instantiate. This feature reminds us that woodblocks cost money and that early modern illustrations were as likely to be symbolic in function as representational. Nonetheless, the application of the same image to different lives and circumstances also seems unusually appropriate to Foxe's agenda. For the book operates according to a logic of repetition and accumulation, by marshaling particulars in the service of a general national history and by translating the particular martyr's life into a general, repeated and repeatable pattern.[33]

An image, finally, could be dysfunctional in the broader sense of upsetting the field of knowledge it was intended to illuminate, of deforming thought. In the context of early empirical science, illustrations could seem most useful for bringing newly observed phenomena, in all their particularity, into view. With respect to natural science, however, Sachiko Kusukawa points out that early illustrations were sometimes treated with suspicion not because they were too little grounded in the empirical but rather because they were too much so: "pictures of natural objects" were seen to be dangerous because they were "portrayals of singular objects, representing all their accidental qualities, but not their substantial forms or essences."[34] In the realm of anatomy, the "variability of the human body" created a problem for illustrative efficacy, because of the gap between particular bodies and the need to present a model or representative body. This was a problem, of course, only if the book was imagined as an object that could substitute for, rather than supplement, practice. Jacques Dubois (Jacobus Sylvius), one of whose medical books is included in this catalog (cat. 24), "used diagrams and illustrations in his lectures," but "doubted they were much use for discovery," since "anatomy had to be practiced by one's own hands as well as eyes, not by merely looking at the body superficially, which is how pictures express the body."[35]

USEFUL CONTINGENCIES: TABULATING THE PARTICULAR

As Kusukawa suggests, the problem of making book forms useful was essentially a problem of particulars. Early modern charts and diagrams of textual content helped organize knowledge into a condensed and memorable spatial form. While such charts are tools rather than substitutes, they nonetheless shape the cognitive process of "placing" particulars and generalizing from them. The tension between a diagram's pedagogical usefulness and its epistemological implications was at the heart of the controversy about the tree diagram that through the influence of Pierre de la Ramée (Petrus Ramus) became immensely popular in a wide range of early modern European texts and genres.[36] Ramus was a philosopher whose importance lay in his pedagogical innovations, which gave priority to the practical utility of knowledge.[37] The synoptic chart was at the center of Ramus's project to make knowledge accessible in the classroom and useful outside it, since its arrangement of complex ideas made them less confusing, easier to remember and hence easier to deploy. The more substantial claim for the table was that it gave visual form to an epistemological method equally applicable, so Ramus claimed, to all disciplinary spheres: method was a disposition of things according to their place in a logical and hierarchical "order of knowledge," so that the dichotomous table's arrangement enabled discovery as the student progressed (left to right) from whole to part, general to specific, antecedent to consequent, known to unknown.[38] Unsurprisingly, critics attacked Ramus's method and spatial divisions as a simplistic model of thought, a reductive substitute for the genuinely rigorous engagement with the generals and particulars that constitute knowledge.

The fold-out Ramist chart that John Dee includes in the 1570 English translation of Euclid's *Elements* (see p. 20) is interesting, however, for the way in which it at once consolidates information and resists the reification that critics feared. As a guide to Dee's elaborate and often unwieldy "Mathematicall Praeface," it extracts and orders the multiple quantitative practices that the preface explores. The spatial economy of the table seduces with the implication of an internal and necessary order among the practices listed, a comprehensive order of use to which Euclid's book itself (which finds its own place in Dee's hierarchy) is subordinated. Dee's table is powerfully oriented to use, in the sense of making his own preface navigable but also in the sense of directing mathematics to practice. So it is notable both that the contemplative ("Principall") branches of mathematics issue at top right in "Use" and that the applied ("Deriuatiue") branches of mathematics issue in a panoply of social practices. The curiously bewildering neologisms that Dee uses to name these practices stand in tension with the clarity that the chart seems to offer. This is a *useful* tension, because it unsettles those readers who might use the chart only to

F. DEE.

Here haue you (according to my promisse) the Groundplat of
my MATHEMATICALL Praface : annexed to *Euclide* (now first)
published in our Englishe tounge. An. 1570. Febr. 3.

Sciences, and Artes Mathematicall, are, either

Principall, which are two, onely,

Arithmetike.

- **Simple,** Which dealeth with Numbers onely : and demonstrateth all their properties and appertenances : where, an Vnit, is Indiuisible.
- **Mixt,** Which with aide of Geometrie principall, demonstrateth some Arithmeticall Conclusion, or Purpose.

Geometrie.

- **Simple,** Which dealeth with Magnitudes, onely : and demonstrateth all their properties, passions, and appertenances : whose Point, is Indiuisible.
- **Mixt,** Which with aide of Arithmetike principall, demonstrateth some Geometricall purpose: as EVCLIDES ELEMENTES.

The vse whereof, is either :

- In thinges Supernaturall, æternall, & Diuine: By Application, Ascending.
- In thinges Mathematicall: without farther Application.
- In thinges Naturall: both Substantiall, & Accidentall, Visible, & Inuisible. &c. By Application: Descending.

The like Vses and Applications are, (though in a degree lower) in the Artes Mathematicall Deriuatiue.

Deriuatiue frō the Principalls: of which, some haue

The names of the Principalls : as,

Arithmetike, *vulgar: which considereth*

- Arithmetike of most vsuall whole Numbers: And of Fractions to them appertaining.
- Arithmetike of Proportions.
- Arithmetike Circular.
- Arithmetike of Radicall Nūbers: Simple, Compound, Mixt: And of their Fractions.
- Arithmetike of Cossike Nūbers: with their Fractions: And the great Arte of Algiebar.

Geometrie, *vulgar: which teacheth Measuring*

At hand
- All Lengthes. ——— Mecometrie.
- All Plaines: As, Land, Borde, Glasse, &c. ——— Embadometrie.
- All Solids: As, Timber, Stone, Vessels, &c. ——— Stereometrie.

With distāce from the thing Measured, as,
- How farre, from the Measurer, any thing is: of him sene, on Land or Water: called **Apomecometrie.**
- How high or deepe, from the leuell of the Measurers standing, any thing is: Seene of hym, on Land or Water: called **Hypsometrie.**
- How broad, a thing is, which is in the Measurers vew : so it be situated on Land or Water : called **Platometrie.**

Of which are growen the Feates & Artes of
- Geodesie : more cunningly to Measure and Suruey Landes, Woods, Waters. &c.
- Geographie.
- Chorographie.
- Hydrographie.
- Stratarithmetrie.

Propre names as,

- **Perspectiue,** Which demonstrateth the maners and properties of all Radiations: Directe, Broken, and Reflected.
- **Astronomie,** Which demonstrateth the Distances, Magnitudes and all Naturall motions, Apparences, and Passions, proper to the Planets and fixed Starres: for any time, past, present, and to come : in respecte of a certaine Horizon, or without respecte of any Horizon.
- **Musike,** Which demonstrateth by reason, and teacheth by sense, perfectly to iudge and order the diuersitie of Soundes, hie or low.
- **Cosmographie,** Which, wholy and perfectly maketh description of the Heauenly, and also Elementall part of the World : and of these partes, maketh homologall application, and mutuall collation necessary.
- **Astrologie,** Which reasonably demonstrateth the operations and effectes of the naturall beames of light, and secrete Influence of the Planets, and fixed Starres, in euery Element and Elementall body : at all times, in any Horizon assigned.
- **Statike,** Which demonstrateth the causes of heauines and lightnes of all thinges : and of the motions and properties to heauines and lightnes belonging.
- **Anthropographie,** Which describeth the Nūber, Measure, Weight, Figure, Situation, and colour of euery diuers thing contained in the perfecte body of MAN : and geueth certaine knowledge of the Figure, Symmetrie, Waight, Characterization, & due Locall motion of any parcell of the seyd body assigned : and of numbers to the said parcell appertaining.
- **Trochilike,** Which demonstrateth the properties of all Circular motions: Simple and Compound.
- **Helicosophie,** Which demonstrateth the designing of all Spirall lines : in Plaine, on Cylinder, Cone, Sphere, Conoid, and Spheroid : and their properties.
- **Pneumatithmie,** Which demonstrateth by close hollow Geometricall figures (Regular and Irregular) the straunge properties (in motion or stay) of the Water, Ayre, Smoke, and Fire, in these Continents, and as they are ioyned to the Elementes next them.
- **Menadrie,** Which demonstrateth, how, aboue Natures Vertue, and power simple : Vertue and force may be multiplied: and so to directe, to lift, to pull to, and to put or cast fro, any multiplied, or simple determined Vertue, Waight, or Force : naturally, not, so, directible, or moueable.
- **Hypogeiodie,** Which demonstrateth, how, vnder the Sphericall Superficies of the Earth, at any depth, to any perpendicular line assigned (whose distance from the perpendiculare of the entrance : and the Azimuth likewise, in respecte of the seyd entrance, is knowen) certaine way, may be prescribed and gone, &c.
- **Hydragogie,** Which demonstrateth the possible leading of Water by Natures law, and by artificiall helpe, from any head (being Spring, standing, or running Water) to any other place assigned.
- **Horometrie,** Which demonstrateth, how, at all times appointed, the precise, vsuall denomination of time, may be knowen, for any place assigned.
- **Zographie,** Which demonstrateth and teacheth, how, the Intersection of all visuall Pyramids, made by any plaine assigned (the Center, distance, and lightes being determined) may be, by lines and proper colours represented.
- **Architecture,** Which is a Science garnished with many doctrines, and diuers Instructions : by whose iudgement, all workes by other workmen finished, are iudged.
- **Nauigation,** Which demonstrateth, how, by the shortest good way, by the aptest direction, and in the shortest time: a sufficient Shippe, betwene any two places (in passage nauigable) assigned, may be conducted: and in all stormes and naturall disturbances chauncing, how to vse the best possible meanes, to recouer the place first assigned.
- **Thaumaturgike,** Which geueth certaine order to make straunge Workes, of the sense to be perceiued: and of men greatly to be wondred at.
- **Archemastrie,** Which teacheth to bring to actuall experience sensible, all worthy conclusions, by all the Artes Mathematicall purposed : and by true Naturall philosophie concluded: And both addeth to them a farder Scope, in the termes of the same Artes: and also, by his proper Method, and in peculiar termes, procedeth, with helpe of the forsayd Artes, to the performance of complete Experiences: which, of no particular Arte, are hable (Formally) to be challenged.

Imprinted by Iohn Day. An. 1570. Feb. 25.

discover what they already know and chiefly because it locates the chart's value in the possibility of an ongoing taxonomic invention. If "Architecture" and "Nauigation" and "Perspectiue" seem familiar as applied mathematical practices, it is not so clear why "Zographie," which "demonstrateth and teacheth, how, the Intersection of all visuall Pyramids . . . may be by lines and proper colours represented," deserves a place on the chart in the same degree. The table, in other words, is less stable than it appears, and that is the point. The entry at the bottom of the table under "Archemastrie" is striking in this regard, not least because it is nearly impossible to determine what Dee is saying:

> Archemastrie, Which teacheth to bring to actuall experience sensible all worthy conclusions, by all the Artes Mathematicall purposed, and by true Naturall philosophie concluded: And both addeth to them a farder Scope, in the terms of the same Artes: and also, by his proper Method, and in peculiar termes, procedeth, with helpe of the forsayd Artes, to the performance of complete Experiences: which, of no particular Arte are hable (Formally) to be challenged.

If Archemastrie (as the ultimate mastery of applied knowledge) is an endpoint for a table oriented toward use, it is also a taxonomic starting point, since it privileges experience, and especially those experiential engagements that escape the tabular scheme because they are in excess of known and "particular Artes." As a model of thought, Dee's Ramist diagram finds a way to accommodate the radical particularity of experience. This is no surprise, since Ramus himself (like Whitney) was so concerned to convert reading into using: understood as a pedagogical tool, his diagrams promised to find room at their edges for the evidence that students might "discover . . . in their own experience" and bring into the domain of authority.[39]

In a different domain, Abraham Fraunce similarly deployed Ramist technology to negotiate the radical particularity of case-by-case thinking in English law. In his 1588 *Lawiers Logike* (cat. 26), Fraunce argued that the law should be taught and written more systematically by demonstrating that the written case reports through which the common law was transmitted were *already* logical. One of the Ramist charts that Fraunce includes in his book digests a single law case by diagramming the logical relation among the case particulars, thereby translating narrative into a visual scheme or "plot."[40] The common lawyers resisted Fraunce's project, as they resisted other attempts explicitly to rationalize the law; the assumption underlying their position was that the law could be taught only as the student's grappling, case by case, with the particulars of legal history that lay (in Fraunce's words) "in volumes confusedly scattered and vtterly vndigested."[41] But Fraunce's rational charts are interesting precisely as an attempt to theorize the case as a genre not of unassimilated particulars, but as particulars already in relation to the general.[42] Indeed, he positions Ramist divisions in opposition to textual forms such as the "vast heaps of scattered discourses, thown into euery corner of our yeare bookes," condemning those who "preferreth the loathsome tossing of an A. B. C. abridgment, before the lightsome perusing of a Methodical coherence of the whole common lawe."[43] Like Dee, Fraunce is concerned to find, in a regularized order, space for the radically particular.

Importantly, Dee's and Fraunce's charts manage particulars in order both to generalize from cultural practices and to imagine those diverse practices as systematic and coherent.[44] Indeed, it is not surprising that they belong to a moment in which disciplinary fields and professions were still in formation.[45] As tools designed to make their respective books more usable, they effectively theorize fields of professional practice (both social and textual) that are not yet fully in place. This is to emphasize the power of format: even when a table seems merely to organize content, it may be making visible something that would other–wise remain submerged. As models for organizing particulars and orienting them toward use, these textual forms anticipate cultural formations.

The Uses of Pleasure

The books featured in *Book Use, Book Theory* are concerned with their own utility, their capacity to instruct. Oriented as they are to language acquisition, practical tasks, social advancement, these are books that might seem removed from the pleasures of reading. But pleasure is integral to how they engage their readers. To return to a book discussed above, it is notable that Alexander Read describes his compilation of anatomical tables and diagrams as a "Manuell" that he hopes "will prooue profitable and delightfull" to his readers. The pairing of the two goals was of course traditional, a version of the Horatian dictum that texts should both "delight and instruct." But beyond the pedagogical or marketing strategy of enticing students and readers to difficult material, this relationship between utility and pleasure can be understood to inform the basic process of textual engagement. We might recall that Read defines his book as effective because it is particularly well fitted to body and mind, so organized as to ease the visual processing of information. His book, he says, "cannot but affoord great *contentment* to the mind" (emphasis added), a formulation that brings together the reader's internalization of textual content and the reader's pleasure. Adrian Johns has emphasized the place of the body and its senses in the process of absorbing information, since early readers "perceived letters on a page through the mediation of their bodies; the passions were the emotional, physiological, and moral responses of the human body to its surroundings, and thus played an unavoidable part in the reading process." Following Johns, we might say that pleasure is part of what he calls the "physiology of reading."[46]

Exemplary here is the pleasure of the how-to book, a genre closely associated with print culture since it was print that made the instructional manual accessible to such a wide range of specialized and non-specialized readers (see Part III). Among others, Elizabeth Eisenstein has emphasized the veritable "flood of treatises" aimed at "would-be autodidacts":

> Even a superficial observer of sixteenth-century literature cannot fail to be impressed by the "avalanche" of treatises which were issued to explain, by a variety of "easy steps," (often supplemented by sharp-edged diagrams) just "how to" draw a picture, compose a madrigal, mix paints, bake clay, keep accounts, survey a field, handle all manner of tools and instruments, work mines, assay metals, move armies or obelisks, design buildings, bridges and machines.[47]

Books of instruction promised to involve readers in the production of their meaning, something that seems integral to the specific pleasure that these books offered, that of taking knowledge, literally and figuratively, into one's own hands, of internalizing and embodying the author's expertise and the expert's authority. Natasha Glaisyer and Sara Pennell point out that early instructional literature often transmitted their knowledge through "dialogue and question and answer formats," which functioned as "a textual approximation of . . . a conversation between the 'expert' and the reader."[48] It is also possible to see such formats in terms of the imaginative pleasures they encouraged by allowing the reader to play both parts, to participate in the making of knowledge by already inhabiting, inside the text, the position of expertise toward which he or she was moving. Courtesy books and other how-tos for social advancement call conspicuous attention to the profit and pleasure of performance.

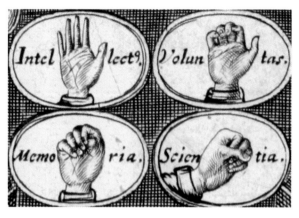

CAT. 36

The reader's pleasure could, of course, destabilize the instruction it was intended to enable. The author of *Aristotle's Master-piece*, an early midwifery guide (cat. 71), worries that the book might in the "Hands of any Obscene or Wanton Person" be turned to pornographic use.[49] Similarly, in his medical guide, Helkiah Crooke is concerned that the illustrated anatomical "Figures" will be seen to be "obscoene as Aretines," an anxiety that Crooke offsets with a proliferation of Latin authorities: "A shameless accusation; for they are no other then those in Vessalius, Plantinus, Platerus, Laurentius, Valverdus, Bauhinus, and the rest."[50] Of course, such warnings could function as an invitation, a guide to the book's own abuse. The fear about "reader response" speaks to the lack of generic distinction between scientific illustration and the pornographic images with which the poet Aretino was associated.

In broader terms, the anxiety around pleasure, and the power of a single reader to undermine a book's authority by turning it to unsanctioned use, was the logical consequence of the fact that early modern reading was so often appropriative. Even the pleasure taken in literature was often a pleasure of appropriation and use. As Randall

Ingram notes, for example, "a volume's signs of aesthetic quality can enhance its practical utility and . . . a volume's signs of practical utility enhance its aesthetic quality."[51] Questioning the distinction between "books for practical use and books for aesthetic appreciation," he points to the well-known practice of commonplacing, through which a reader mined a text for expressions to be used later on his or her own terms.[52] Working with a copy of John Donne's 1633 *Poems* in which an early reader has added an extraordinary index of useful categories, Ingram writes that the book's owner "seems much less concerned with how Donne might express his own subjectivity than with how these 'expressions' might be taken from Donne's book and used in some other personalized context."[53] When an "aesthetic" text becomes useful in this way, a how-to for self-expression, readers become primary in the process of converting one kind of authority, the author's or the text's, into another, their own. As Richard Helgerson has noted, "Intended to represent the power of the authorial self, print ends by empowering the consumers of that representation. Print makes readers kings."[54]

The pleasure readers took specifically in literature was seen as dangerous for producing uncontrollable social agents.[55] Vernacular romances, which printers made widely available for a burgeoning book market, were consistently attacked, for example, for fostering idleness, licentiousness and dangerous flights of imagination. Such books were understood to be particularly dangerous for women, a point that the Protestant reformer Heinrich Bullinger makes in his book on Christian matrimony:

> let them avoyde idlenes, be occupied ether doing some profytable thynge for youre familie, or els redynge some godly boke, let them not read bokes of fables of fonde & lyght loue . . . Bokes of Robyn hode, Beves of Hampton, Troilus, & such lyke fables do but kyndle in lyers lyke lyes and wanton loue, which ought not in yought [youth] with theyr fyrst spettle [spittle] to be dronke in, lest they euer remayne in them.[56]

Similarly, the Spanish humanist Juan Luis Vives catalogs romances from Spain, France, Flanders and England as "vngracious bokes" written by "idell menne."[57] He warns that such texts, and all such books that women read "to kepe them self in the thoughtes of loue" can only lead to vice; *as books* they threaten chastity by invading the body through eye and ear: "It were better for them nat only to haue no lernynge at all, but also to lese theyr eies, that they shulde nat rede: and theyr eares, that they shulde nat here."[58] For Vives, to "haue pleasure in these bokes" is a form of "madness." This pleasure is so far from valuable that Vives imagines the practical uses of such books only in terms of a mock how-to book, a book for bawds: "Also there is no wytte in them, but a fewe wordes of wanton luste . . . . And if they be redde but for this, the best were to make bokes of baudes craftes: for in other thynges, what crafte can be hadde of suche a maker, that is ignorant of all good crafte?"[59]

Even fictions taught within a sanctioned institutional context caused anxiety around questions of pleasure and use.[60] The humanists placed classical literature at the center of the grammar school curriculum, so that boys learned Latin by reading, for example, the comedies of Terence (cat. 11–14), and mastered eloquence through the poetry of Horace and Ovid.[61] Richard Halpern has pointed out that humanist educators who turned to poetry and plays to teach language use and good style were deeply concerned about the content, particularly the erotic content, of the texts they used. "Humanist pedagogy," he writes, "tried to solve the problem of poetic content by treating poetry as a source of *copia*, or elocutionary richness," thereby separating style from content, or, to put this another way, the useful from the pleasurable dimensions of literature.[62] Paradoxically, such a split produces a version of literariness grounded in the very pleasure that literary study would exile.[63]

It is perhaps because their own status in respect of use is in question that early literary texts so often represent books as either dangerous or deceptive. No text embraces the errancy of reading pleasure more fully than *Don Quixote*, with its representation of Quixote's allegiance to the norms of the chivalric romances he has read. A product of book consumption, he simultaneously encounters his own origins in the collective process of book *production*, when, as Roger Chartier has emphasized, he engages with the very printers, correctors and translators who have made him and sent him wandering into the world. Chartier brilliantly reads *Don Quixote* as resisting both the idealization that would eclipse the material conditions of textual production and the alternative that would privilege "the materiality of symbolic productions at the expense of their meaning."[64] Cervantes's text, in other words, offers a lesson on the irreducible relationship between historical and theoretical accounts of book use.

English drama is similarly self-conscious about book use, perhaps because books were used in the making of plays, whether as classical or contemporary source texts or as the promptbook through which a theatrical company adapted a written play for oral performance (see cat. 6). It is no surprise that when books are used on stage as props, they are so often foregrounded *as* props, useful not only for the actor's performance but the character's too. Examples include *Hamlet*, in which Polonius gives Ophelia a prop with which to deceive Hamlet: "Read on this book, / That show of such an exercise may color / Your loneliness" (3.1.43–45);[65] *Richard III*, in which, as part of the performative strategy that will bring him to the throne, Richard appears before the aldermen of London, with "a book of prayer in his hand" (3.7.97); and John Webster's *The Duchess of Malfi,* in which a Bible functions as a weapon laced with poison, which the Cardinal of Aragon encourages Julia, his mistress, to "Kiss" (5.2.272), thereby killing her through a devotional gesture.[66] The abuse of the book here vividly grounds the play's anti-Catholicism by transforming the Bible into a material vector, a perverse version of the rituals of mediation that Protestants attacked as idolatrous. Crucially, in all of these cases, the book is used to deceive, displacing onto the material book the usual criticism leveled against theater as being morally useless or, indeed, so pleasurable as to be a "schoole of abuse" for the inciting of vice.[67]

In absorbing and redirecting to dramatic effect the accusations leveled against the theater and against fiction, these texts make use of their own uselessness and potential for abuse. In *The Tempest*, famously, Prospero's overuse or misuse of his books and library has been the cause of his downfall and exile from Milan. Just as his library became a dangerous substitute for the state ("my library / was Dukedom large enough" [1.109–110]), so his retreat into the "volumes / I prize above my dukedom" (1.2.167–68) substituted for a practical civic consciousness. In the fantasy space of the island, on the other hand, his books enable him to govern and control its inhabitants: "Without them" Caliban says, "He's but a sot" (3.2.92–93). If Prospero's books in Milan were useless for action and practice, as Jeffrey Masten points out, they "enable authority" on the island by grounding his ability to act and to direct the actions of others.[68] Paradoxically, then, while the play allows him to leave Milan with the books that were ineffectual for rule, he must abandon the book that has been useful to him, specifically by dissolving it into another medium: "And deeper than did ever plummet sound / I'll drown my book" (5.1.56–57). The book's use-value is so powerful it must be left behind, consigned to depths that invert the reach of its textual effects.

Montaigne, whose *Essais* (cat. 30) testify to his attachment to his library and to his use of the books he read, similarly notes the power of leaving books behind: "When I write I prefer to do without the company and remembrance of books, for fear that they may interfere with my style."[69] Books are useful, have force, only when they are digested for reuse. Throughout the *Essais*, Montaigne describes his own reading in these terms, as, for example, when he notes the advantage of books composed in short sections, a format that allows them easily to be reused, the passages re-arranged in response to Montaigne's arrangement of his evolving self:

> As for my other reading, which mingles a little more profit with the pleasure, and by which I learn to arrange my humors and my ways, the books that serve me for this are Plutarch, since he exists in French, and Seneca. Both have this notable advantage for my humor, that the knowledge I seek is there treated in detached pieces that do not demand the obligation of long labor, of which I am incapable. . . . For they have no continuity from one to the other.[70]

Montaigne's selective absorption and arrangement of these already "detached pieces" locates the "profit" of reading not in the "obligation of long labor," but in the pleasures of appropriation, through which he creates a complex self whose discontinuities mirror the structure of the texts read.

In contrast to his own active engagements, Montaigne satirizes those who merely read books without using and consuming them, those who fail, as it were, to allow textual authority to vanish in the process of self-assertion. Pedants, or "little men of learning," he writes, are merely "lettre-ferus (letter struck), men whom letters have dealt a hammer blow," [71] as though they were themselves the lettered page that they engage only on the surface. The pedant is *bookish*, furthermore, not in the positive sense in which Montaigne says of himself that, "reader, I am myself the matter of my book,"[72] but in the sense of being someone who, "when I ask him what he knows, asks me for a book in order to point it out to me."[73] If the pedant merely props himself up with books rather than internalizing them, for Montaigne the traditional practice of making books useful by digesting them becomes a vehicle for a new kind of selfhood. In the idea that a book becomes most useful, most productive, when it is no longer visible as the tool or instrument that has served you, when it is hidden from others (and quite possibly even from you) as the origin of the authority it gave you, Montaigne theorizes book use as a continual and unending vanishing. It is in this space, where books become part of you becoming yourself, that reading and use are both experienced as pleasure.

NOTES

1. Geffrey Whitney, *A Choice of Emblemes* (Leiden, 1586), 171. The illustration of the emblem is taken from Henry Green, ed., *Whitney's "Choice of Emblemes": A Fac-simile Reprint* (London: Lovell Reeve, 1866).

2. Anthony Grafton and Lisa Jardine, *From Humanism to the Humanities: Education and the Liberal Arts in Fifteenth- and Sixteenth-Century Europe* (Cambridge: Harvard University Press, 1986), 163–64. Grafton and Jardine are speaking here of the importance of "utility" in the new philosophy of Rudolf Agricola and Desiderius Erasmus.

3. On the temporality of prudence, see, for example, Cicero, *De Inventione*, trans. H.M. Hubbell, Loeb Classical Library (Cambridge: Harvard University Press, 1949), II.lii.160, p. 327. Thomas Hobbes distinguishes between prudence and wisdom in chapter 5 of the *Leviathan*: "For though wee usually have one name of Wisedome for them both; yet the Latines did always distinguish between *Prudentia* and *Sapientia;* ascribing the former to Experience, the later to Science." By "science," Hobbes means theoretical as opposed to practical knowledge. See *Leviathan*, ed. C. B. Macpherson (1651; Harmondsworth: Penguin, 1968), 117.

4. On writing and the materiality of memory, see Jonathan Goldberg, *Writing Matter: From the Hands of the English Renaissance* (Stanford: Stanford University Press, 1990).

5. The analysis of early readers' marks and marginalia now occupies an important place in the history of the book. Recent studies include William H. Sherman, "What Did Renaissance Readers Write in Their Books?" in *Books and Readers in Early Modern England: Material Studies*, ed. Jennifer Andersen and Elizabeth Sauer (Philadelphia: University of Pennsylvania Press, 2002); Stephen Orgel, "Margins of Truth," in *The Renaissance Text: Theory, Editing, Textuality*, ed. Andrew Murphy (Manchester: University of Manchester Press, 2000); Steven Zwicker, "Reading the Margins: Politics and the Habits of Appropriation," in *Refiguring Revolutions: Aesthetics and Politics from the English Revolution to the Romantic Revolution*, ed. Kevin Sharpe and Steven Zwicker (Berkeley: University of California Press, 1998); and Monique Hulvey, "Not So Marginal: Manuscript Annotations in The Folger Incunabula," *Papers of the Bibliographical Society of America* 92.2 (June 1998): 159–76. The personal nature of marginalia necessarily amplifies the historical importance of the individual case study, a fact reflected in the literature. See, for example, Kevin Sharpe, *Reading Revolutions: The Politics of Reading in Early Modern England* (New Haven: Yale University Press, 2000); Anthony Grafton, "Is the History of Reading a Marginal Enterprise? Guillaume Budé and His Books," *Papers of the Bibliographical Society of America* 91.2 (June 1997): 139–57; William H. Sherman, *John Dee: The Politics of Reading and Writing in the English Renaissance* (Amherst: University of Massachusetts Press, 1995); and Lisa Jardine and Anthony Grafton, "Studied for Action: How Gabriel Harvey Read His Livy," *Past and Present* 129 (November 1990): 30–78.

6. For the textual construction of authorship, see Wendy Wall, *The Imprint of Gender: Authorship and Publication in the English Renaissance* (Ithaca: Cornell University Press, 1993).

7. *Imitatio Christi* [Cologne, 1503]. This book, held at the Catholic University of America library, is described and illustrated in *The Reader Revealed*, ed. Sabrina Alcorn Baron, Elizabeth Walsh and Susan Scola (Washington: Folger Shakespeare Library, 2001), 109–110. The catalog is a valuable introduction to the relationship between early modern books and their readers.

8. Thomas Hariot, *A briefe and true report of the new found land of Virginia* (London, 1588), E4r–v. The 1590 edition of the text is reprinted in facsimile in Hariot, *A briefe and true report,* intro. Paul Hulton (New York: Dover, 1972), 27.

9. For an account of Hariot and this passage in particular, see Stephen Greenblatt's "Invisible Bullets," chap. 2, *Shakespearean Negotiations: The Circulation of Social Energy in Renaissance England* (Berkeley: University of California Press, 1988), 21–65.

10. We thank Eric Slauter for this point.

11. Greenblatt, "Invisible Bullets," 31.

12. Mary Rowlandson, *The Sovereignty and Goodness of God*, ed. Neal Salisbury (1682; Boston: Bedford Books, 1997), 90.

13. Ann Rosalind Jones and Peter Stallybrass, "Fetishisms and Renaissances," *Historicism, Psychoanalysis, and Early Modern Culture*, ed. Carla Mazzio and Douglas Trevor (New York: Routledge, 2000), 21. Jones and Stallybrass's investigation of early modern objects in terms of fetishism draws on William Pietz's argument that the idea of the fetish, later taken up by Marx and Freud, originated in a sixteenth-century context as a way for European colonists to denigrate animistic beliefs among West African peoples. See William Pietz, "The Problem of the Fetish, I," *Res* 9 (Spring 1985), 5–17.

14. "Sacris quidem literis vbique prima debetur autoritas, sed tamen ego non-nunquam offendo quaedam vel dicta a veteribus vel scripta ab Ethnicis, etiam poetis, tam caste, tam sancte, tam diuinitus, vt mihi non possim persuadere, quin pectus illorum, quum illa scriberent, numen aliquod bonum agitauerit . . . . Fateor affectum meum apud amicos; non possum legere librum Ciceronis de Senectute, de Amicitia, de Officiis, de Tusculanis quaestionibus, quin aliquoties exosculer codicem . . . ." See Desiderius Erasmus, "Convivium Religiosum," *Colloquia*, ed. L.-E. Halkin et al., in *Opera Omnia*, I, 3 (Amsterdam: North-Holland, 1972), 251. The translation has been adapted from "The Godly Feast," *The Colloquies*, trans. Craig R. Thompson (Chicago: University of Chicago Press, 1965), 65.

15. Peter Stallybrass, "Fingers and Books," delivered as the Paul Gottschalk Lecture, Cornell University, 1999; and "Scrolls and Books: Navigating the Bible," in Andersen and Sauer, *Books and Readers in Early Modern England*, 51.

16. Alexander Read, *Somatographia Anthropine. Or A Description of the Body of Man* (London, 1616), A3r. The illustration from Read's text in our introduction is taken from the 1634 edition published by Thomas Cotes, which replicates the illustrations and format of the 1616 first edition.

17. Read, *Somatographia*, A3v.

18. On the relationship between word and image in medieval mnemonic systems, see Mary Carruthers and Jan. M. Ziolkowski, *The Medieval Craft of Memory: An Anthology of Texts and Pictures* (Philadelphia: University of Pennsylvania Press, 2003).

19. Helkiah Crooke, *Mikrokosmographia: A Description of the Body of Man* (London, 1615), ¶2v. The copy of Crooke in this catalog (cat. 70) is a later edition.

20. Ibid., ¶2v.

21. On the professions of law and medicine in relation to textual learning, see especially Ian Maclean, *Interpretation and Meaning in the Renaissance: The Case of Law* (Cambridge: Cambridge University Press, 1992); and *Logic, Signs and Nature in the Renaissance: The Case of Learned Medicine* (Cambridge: Cambridge University Press, 2002).

22. Roger Ascham, *The Scholemaster*, (London, 1570), 43r.

23. Edward Coke, *Le Quart Part des Reportes del Edward Coke Chiualier* (London, 1604), B3v.

24. Francis Bacon, *Works*, ed. James Spedding et al., 14 vols. (London 1857–74), vol. 9, 25–6. Cited in Peter Beal, "Notions in Garrison," *New Ways of Looking at Old Texts*, ed. W. Speed Hill (Binghampton: Renaissance English Text Society, 1993), 138.

25. Ann Blair, "Annotating and Indexing Natural Philosophy," *Books and the Sciences in History*, ed. Marina Frasca-Spada and Nick Jardine (Cambridge: Cambridge University Press, 2000), 69–89.

26. Neil Rhodes and Jonathan Sawday, "Paperworlds: Imagining the Renaissance Computer," *The Renaissance Computer: Knowledge Technology in the First Age of Print*, ed. Neil Rhodes and Jonathan Sawday (New York: Routledge, 2000), 7.

27. Stephen Orgel, "Records of Culture," Afterword, in Andersen and Sauer, *Books and Readers in Early Modern England*, 286–87.

28. The index in the 1651 sixth edition included in the catalogue is on leaves Zzzz4r–Aaaaa4r.

29. Richard Strier, "Self-Consumption," chap. 2, *Resistant Structures: Particularity, Radicalism, and Renaissance Texts* (Berkeley: University of California Press, 1995), 41. Strier's essay takes issue with Stanley Fish's account of Burton's text in *Self-Consuming Artifacts: The Experience of Seventeenth-Century Literature* (Berkeley: University of California Press, 1972).

30. As an index of printing errors, indeed, the errata sheet makes visible the process of creating textual authority over time. The errata sheet, as Seth Lerer has noted, could highlight the reader's own authority in relation to the text, since it makes visible that "the early book is always a work in progress and in process, a text intruded upon for emendation, a text that invites the correction of the reader. There is nothing like an errata sheet to prompt the reader to seek out yet more errata—that is, nothing like the admission of *some* errors to provoke us to believe that the work is *full* of errors." See his "Errata: Mistakes and Masters in the Early Modern Book," chap. 1, *Error and the Academic Self: The Scholarly Imagination, Medieval to Modern* (New York: Columbia University Press, 2002), 18.

31. Thomas N. Corns, "The Early Modern Search Engine: Indices, Title Pages, Marginalia and Contents," in Rhodes and Sawday, *The Renaissance Computer,* 97.

32. Stephen Orgel, "Textual Icons: Reading Early Modern Illustrations," in Rhodes and Sawday, *The Renaissance Computer,* 60, 63–64.

33. Writing on Foxe, Steven Mullaney reminds us of the politics involved in making a case exemplary, in making it fully part of the imagined community that Foxe means to create. See his "Reforming Resistance: Class, Gender, and Legitimacy in Foxe's *Book of Martyrs,*" in *Print, Manuscript, and Performance: The Changing Relations of the Media in Early Modern England*, ed. Arthur Marotti and Michael Bristol (Columbus: Ohio State University Press, 2000).

34. Sachiko Kusukawa, "Illustrating Nature," in Frasca-Spada and Jardine, *Books and the Sciences in History*, 107.

35. Kusukawa, "Illustrating Nature," 108. See also Nancy Siraisi, "Vesalius and Human Diversity in *De Humani Corporis Fabrica,*" *Journal of the Warburg and Courtauld Institutes* 57 (1994): 60–88.

36. Ramus did not in fact invent the visual format that carries his name: the dichotomous table was "frequently seen in the earlier age of manuscripts, and favoured by medical authors who published before Ramus." See Brian Copenhaver and Charles Schmitt, *A History of Western Philosophy 3: Renaissance Philosophy* (Oxford: Oxford University Press, 1992), 238. Cited in Ian Maclean, "Logical Division and Visual Dichotomies: Ramus in the Context of Legal and Medical Writing," in *The Influence of Petrus Ramus*, ed. Mordechai Feingold, Joseph Freedman and Wolfgang Rother (Basel: Schwabe and Co, 2001), 229.

37. See Grafton and Jardine, *From Humanism to the Humanities,* 168.

38. Petrus Ramus, *Dialectica A. Talaei praelectionibus illustrata* (Basel, 1569), 465–66. Cited in Walter Ong, *Ramus, Method, and the Decay of Dialogue* (Cambridge: Harvard University Press, 1958), 248–49.

39. Kenneth Knoespel, "The Narrative Matter of Mathematics John Dee's Preface to the Elements of Euclid of Megara (1570)," *Philological Quarterly* 66 (1987): 33.

40. William Sherman notes the close connection between the Ramist chart and the practically oriented political treatises that went under the name of "plat" or "plot." See his "Anatomizing the Commonwealth: Language, Politics and the Elizabethan Political Order," in *The Project of Prose in Early Modern Europe and the New World*, ed. Elizabeth Fowler and Roland Greene (Cambridge: Cambridge University Press, 1997), 109.

41. Abraham Fraunce, *The Lawiers Logicke* (London, 1588), ¶3v. On Fraunce's book as an exemplary failure to bring the common law into conversation with other discourses, see Peter Goodrich, *Languages of Law: From Logics of Memory to Nomadic Masks* (London: Weidenfeld and Nicolson, 1990), 15–43; and "*Ars Bablativa*: Ramism, Rhetoric, and the Genealogy of English Jurisprudence," in *Legal Hermeneutics: History, Theory and Practice*, ed. Gregory Leyh (Berkeley: University of California Press, 1992).

42. Relevant here is James Chandler's remark that "the word *case*, as its root suggests, has to do with falls and befallings, with the world of chance and contingency and with the positing of worlds—normative orders—against which chance and contingency might be established as such." See his *England in 1819: The Politics of Literary Culture and the Case of Romantic Historicism* (Chicago: University of Chicago Press, 1998), 39–40.

43. Fraunce, *The Lawiers Logicke*, 119v.

44. In *The Counter-Renaissance* (New York: Harcourt, Brace & World, 1950), Hyram Haydn remarks that the early modern period is marked by the "ultimate desertion of the universal for the particular" (143). The problem of the particular in relationship to "coherent" fields of knowledge and practice is by no means a phenomenon specific to scientific and legal books. "History," according to a character named "Memory" in a 1607 university drama, is so rife with particularities that he can no longer remember anything: "A dog cannot piss in a Noblemans shoe, but it must be sprinkled into the Chronicles, so that I never could remember my Treasure more full, & never emptier of honorable, and true heroycall Actions." See Thomas Tomkis, *Lingua: Or the Combat of the Tongue and the Five Senses for Superiority* (London, 1607), D1.

45. In the case of Fraunce, it is highly suggestive that his book draws examples of logical thinking from Edmund Spenser's 1579 *Shepheardes Calender* and that one of his Ramist diagrams digests into tabular form one of Virgil's eclogues. The latter exercise was modeled on the work of Ramus's student Thomas Freige, who in his *XII Virgili Aeneidos libros tabulae* (Basle, 1587) had reduced the *Aeneid* to Ramist charts. The relevant point is not just that Fraunce means to entertain his readers with material that is less dry than the law, but that law and poetry were closer in this period than they are now.

46. Adrian Johns, "The Physiology of Reading: Print and the Passions," chap. 6, *The Nature of the Book: Print and Knowledge in the Making* (Chicago: University of Chicago Press, 1998), 386. For an analysis of the personalized and "embodied" author a reader might encounter, see Douglas Bruster, "The Structural Transformation of Print in Late Elizabethan England," in Marotti and Bristol, *Print, Manuscript, and Performance*, 49–89.

47. Elizabeth Eisenstein, *The Printing Press as an Agent of Change: Communications and Cultural Transformations in Early-Modern Europe* (Cambridge: Cambridge University Press, 1979), 243–44. For recent approaches to the place of instructional literature in early modern English culture, see Natasha Glaisyer and Sara Pennell, eds., *Didactic Literature in England, 1500–1800: Expertise Constructed* (Aldershot: Ashgate, 2003).

48. Glaisyer and Pennell, "Introduction," in *Didactic Literature in England,* 13.

49. Aristotle, pseud. *Aristotle's Master-piece: Or, The Secrets of Generation* (London: n.p., 1692), A4v.

50. Crooke, *Mikrokosmographia,* ¶2v.

51. Randall Ingram, "Seventeenth-Century Didactic Readers, Their Literature, and Ours," in Glaisyer and Pennell, *Didactic Literature in England,* 63.

52. For commonplaces as cultural capital in the context of social mobility, see Mary Thomas Crane, *Framing Authority: Sayings, Self, and Society in Sixteenth-Century England* (Princeton: Princeton University Press, 1993). For an extended analysis of commonplacing as a print phenomenon, see Ann Moss, *Printed Commonplace-Books and the Structuring of Renaissance Thought* (Oxford: Clarendon Press, 1996). Continuous with the process of commonplacing poetic texts is the copying of poems themselves into commonplace books and miscellanies. For the manuscript circulation of poetry within print culture, see Arthur Marotti, *Manuscript, Print and the English Renaissance Lyric* (Ithaca: Cornell University Press, 1995). An interesting case study is Victoria Burke, "Women and Early Seventeenth-Century Manuscript Culture: Four Miscellanies," *Seventeenth Century* 12 (1997): 135–50.

53. Ingram, "Seventeenth-Century Didactic Readers," 67.

54. Richard Helgerson, "Milton Reads the King's Book: Print, Performance, and the Making of a Bourgeois Idol," *Criticism* 29 (1987): 6. For an interesting example of just how different the "how-to books" made by different readers of a single book could be, see Glaisyer and Pennell, "Introduction," 3: Whereas a Staffordshire owner of Thomas Blundeville's *The foure chiefest Offices belonging to Horsemanship* (1st ed.1566) used it as a highly practical book, adding "manuscript recipes for treating equine diseases," the Cambridge scholar Gabriel Harvey annotated his copy so as to underscore "fine turns of phrase as well as pieces of good advice; in his summary written in the front of the book, Harvey praised the book, not for its practicality but for its celebration of the chivalry of the warrior."

55. For an extensive analysis of the problem of literary pleasure in relation to the classical ideal of moderation as reimagined in the Renaissance, see Joshua Scodel, *Excess and the Mean in Early Modern English Literature* (Princeton: Princeton University Press, 2002).

56. Heinrich Bullinger, *The Christen state of Matrimonye . . . Translated by Myles Couerdale* (London, 1541), 75r–v. Partially cited in Helen Hackett, *Women and Romance Fiction in the English Renaissance* (Cambridge: Cambridge University Press, 2000), 10.

57. Juan Luis Vives, *A very frutefull and pleasant boke called the Instruction of a Christen Woman . . . turned out of Laten into Englysshe by Rycharde Hyrd* (London, 1529), E4r–v.

58. Ibid., E3v.

59. Ibid., E4v.

60. For the status and circulation of vernacular poetry, see Arthur Marotti, *John Donne: Coterie Poet* (Madison: University of Wisconsin Press, 1986): "lyric poetry was basically a genre for gentleman-amateurs who regarded their literary 'toys' as ephemeral works . . . as trifles to be transmitted in manuscript within a limited social world . . ." (3).

61. On humanist teaching, see Grafton and Jardine, *From Humanism to the Humanities;* T. W. Baldwin, *William Shakespere's Small Latine & Lesse Greeke* (Urbana: University of Illinois Press, 1944); and Rebecca Bushnell, *A Culture of Teaching: Early Modern Humanism in Theory and Practice* (Ithaca: Cornell University Press, 1996).

62. Richard Halpern, *The Poetics of Primitive Accumulation* (Ithaca: Cornell University Press, 1991), 47.

63. Indeed, Sir Philip Sidney, as Mary Ellen Lamb has emphasized, comes to defend poetry by recuperating pleasure as useful in the moral domain. See her "Apologizing for Pleasure in Sidney's 'Apology for Poetry': The Nurse of Abuse Meets the Tudor Grammar School," *Criticism* 36 (1994): 499–519.

64. Roger Chartier, "The Written Word at the Age of Its Technical Reproducibility," (lecture, Warwick Humanities Research Center, May 8, 2003), http://www2.warwick.ac.uk/fac/arts/hrc/arch/lectures/chartiertext.

65. All citations of Shakespeare plays are to *The Riverside Shakespeare*, ed. G. Blakemore Evans (Boston: Houghton Mifflin, 1997).

66. John Webster, *The Duchess of Malfi and Other Plays*, ed. René Weis (Oxford: Oxford University Press, 1996).

67. Stephen Gosson, *The schoole of abuse* (London, 1587). On the antitheatrical tradition, see Jonas Barish, *The Antitheatrical Prejudice* (Berkeley: University of California Press, 1981).

68. Jeffrey Masten, "Representing Authority: Patriarchalism, Absolutism, and the Author on Stage," chap. 3, *Textual Intercourse: Collaboration, Authorship, and Sexualities in Renaissance Drama* (Cambridge: Cambridge University Press, 1997), 109.

69. "Quand j'escris, je me passe bien de la compagnie et souvenance des livres, de peur qu'ils n'interrompent ma forme." See Michel de Montaigne, "Sur des vers de Virgile," *Les Essais de Montaigne*, ed. P. Villey (Paris: Presses Universitaires de France, 1978), III, 5, 874B. The translation is from "On some verses of Virgil," *The Complete Essays of Montaigne*, trans. Donald M. Frame (Stanford: Stanford University Press, 1958), III, 5, 666B.

70. "Quant à mon autre leçon, qui mesle un peu plus de fruit au plaisir, par où j'apprens à renger mes humeurs et mes conditions, les livres qui m'y servent, c'est Plutarque, dépuis qu'il est François, et Seneque. Ils ont tous deux cette notable commodité pour mon humeur, que la science que j'y cherche, y est traictée à pieces décousues, qui ne demandent pas l'obligation d'un long travail, dequoy de suis incapable . . . . Car elles n'ont point de suite des unes aux autres." See Montaigne, "Des livres," *Les Essais,* II, 10, 413A. The translation is from "On books," *The Complete Essays*, II, 10, 300A.

71. "Mon vulgaire Perigordin appelle fort plaisamment "Lettreferits" ces sçaventeaux, comme si vous disiez "lettre-ferus," ausquels les lettres ont donné un coup de marteau, comme on dict." See Montaigne, "Du pedantisme," *Les Essais,* I, 25, 139A. The translation is from "Of pedantry," *The Complete Essays,* I, 25, 102A.

72. "Ainsi, lecteur, je suis moy-mesmes la matiere de mon livre." Montaigne, "Au Lecteur," *Les Essais,* 3A. The translation is from "To the Reader," *The Complete Essays,* 3A.

73. "J'en cognoy, à qui quand je demande ce qu'il sçait, il me demande un livre pour me le montrer; et n'oserait me dire qu'il a le derriere galeux, s'il ne va sur le champ estudier et son lexicon, que c'est que galeux, et que c'est que derriere." See Montaigne, "Du pedantisme," *Les Essais,* I, 25, 137C. The translation is from "Of pedantry," *The Complete Essays,* I, 25, 101C.

LVCII ANNEI SENECAE COR-
dubensis de moribus liber vnus.

Mne peccatum actio est. Actio autem omnis voluntaria est, tam honesta quàm turpis. ergo voluntarium est omne peccatum. Tolle excusatione, nemo peccat inuitus. Educatio & disciplina mores faciunt: & id vnusquisque sapit, quod didicit. Itaque bona consuetudo excutere debet, quod mala instruxit. Nihil interest quo animo facias, quod fecisse vitiosum est: quia facta cernutur, animus vero no videtur. Nulla autem laus est, non facere quod facere non possis. Quid homini est inimicissimum? homo. Libeter feras, quod necesse est: Dolor patientia vincitur. Expecta quo nuquam poeniteas. Non quam multis placeas, sed qualibus, stude. In hoc tantum incumbe, vt libetius audias, quàm loquaris. Multos vitam differetes, mors iuncta prauenit. Itaq; omnis dies velut vltimus iudicetur. Tristitia, si potes, ne admiseris: sin minus, ne ostenderis. Amicos secreto admone, palam autem lauda. Verba rebus non personis æstimanda sunt. Oratorem te puta, si tibi ante omnes quod oportet persuaseris. Vt licentiosa mancipia animi imperio coërce, linguam, vetrem, & libidinem. Quod tacitum esse velis, nemini dixeris. Si tibi non imperasti, quomodo ab alio siletium speras? Ridiculum est, aliquem odio nocentis, innocentiam perdere. Monstro similis est auaritia senilis. Quid enim stultius est, quod dici solet, quam via deficiente viaticum augere? Omnes infantes terra nudos excipit. Non pudet te fortius nasci quàm viuere? Quid dulcius quàm habere amicum, cum quo audeas

A. ij

Technologies of Use

CLUES TO BOOK USE in the early modern period are found in the marks that readers left in and on their books. Using a book meant making it one's own, often by annotating it, binding it, or putting it to use in particular and sometimes surprising contexts. A printed book, moreover, can itself tell us about the strategies of use required for it to accomplish its meaning.

Part I, "Technologies of Use," explores the ways in which a book's forms anticipated, enabled and sometimes determined particular kinds of use. (To take a simple example, a small book asks to be held and maybe carried: a pocket book is at once a textual form and a category of use.) Features of the book now often taken for granted, like the title page or page layout, were in this period more clearly understood to be interpretive guides, either by implying a use or by actually guiding the eye through typographical variation or the arrangement of words on the page. A feature like illustration, although sometimes only ornamental, could constitute a sophisticated technology of use. Scientific illustrations, for example, had a range of functions: they attested to the diffusion of new technologies (such as the microscope); they enabled the reader to "see" textual information and the material world in a new way; and they worked aesthetically and commercially by heightening the visual pleasure offered by the book.

Using books implies an active and productive engagement with them. Indeed, use *per se* poses a challenge to the book's authority and integrity, not only in terms of torn pages, broken spines and missing covers, but also because a reader's use makes him or her integral to the production of meaning. In this respect, it is possible to see that when books presented themselves as conspicuous wholes (an author's "Works" or corpus, for example, or the Bible understood as *the* book), they were in some sense protecting themselves against use, by asking instead to be read.

DETAIL, CAT. 5

Making Books, Using Books

1 Albrecht Dürer
(1471–1528)
Vnderweysung der Messung
[Nüremberg: n.p.], 1525
Rare Book Collection,
Joseph Halle Schaffner Bequest

The three texts in this section exemplify particular relationships between books and their users. Albrecht Dürer's *Vnderweysung der Messung* (*The Art of Measurement*, cat. 1), one of the most celebrated early manuals for artists and craftsmen, imagines readers as users, insofar as it consistently directs them, through illustration and textual narration, to perform tasks and so apprehend theory through practice. The illustration reproduced demonstrates how to draw a solid object and its shadow. The paper foldout is required for the representation of perspectival distance. But by placing the human figure, the implied reader or user, outside the book, the illustration is also paradigmatic of how early books imagined their users moving beyond them.

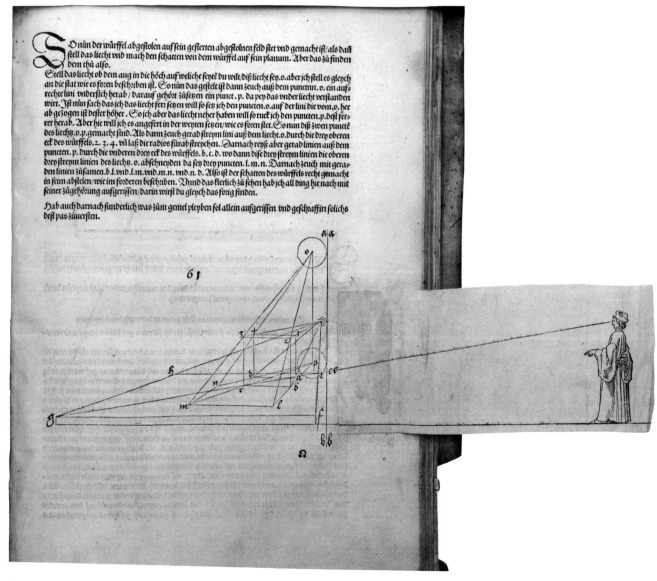

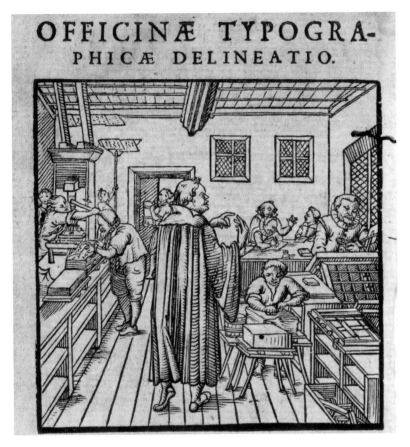

2 Hieronymus Hornschuch
(1573–1616)
Orthotypographia
Leipzig: Michaël Lantzenberger
excudebat, 1608
Rare Book Collection,
Berlin Collection

For a book to be usable, it must of course be legible. Hieronymus Hornschuch's *Orthotypographia* (cat. 2) was the first technical manual for printers, specifically for correctors, those hired by the printing house to proofread the individual sheets of a book. Hornschuch's manual for regularizing production aimed both to eliminate error and make books clearer and thus more usable; at the same time, it demonstrates how a book could be subject to use even during the process of making it. The proofreaders' marks that Hornschuch illustrates vanish from the corrected page and the printed book, rendering the process of correction all but invisible in the historical archive of early print. Hornschuch's *printed* marks remind us, then, that the corrector's manuscript marks, though seldom preserved, were integral to the making of books: proofreading is on a continuum with the reading it facilitates, evincing a highly practical (if conventional) engagement, on the part of a specific kind of reader, with an author's text.

3 Giovanni Battista Cacace
   (fl. 1650)
   Theatrvm Omnivm Scientiarivm
   Naples: Robertus Mollus
   Typographus Excudebat, 1650
   Rare Book Collection

Drawn from Giovanni Battista Cacace's collection of emblems on the arts and sciences (cat. 3), the illustration for pharmaceutical knowledge suggestively positions book use as a collaboration involving a tension between making books and, it would appear, consuming them.

Marking Books

4 *The Holy Bible*
    London: by Bonham Norton
    and Iohn Bill, 1627
    Rare Book Collection,
    Maurice H. Grant Collection
    of British Bibles

One way to mark a book is to write one's name in it. This is a sign of identification, ownership, property, but not necessarily use. The three texts illustrated here carry evidence of ownership and also of private and public use. The cover of the small seventeenth-century Bible (cat. 4) was embroidered, and its front edge elaborately decorated, possibly by the women of an Anglican community at Little Gidding, which ran a well-known bindery that concentrated on Bibles and devotional works. Given that books in this period were often bought unbound, a binding could indicate the owner's economic status and his or her (as opposed to the author's) sense of the book. This binding is unusually expressive of the owner's relation to the book as a precious object for devotional use.

4

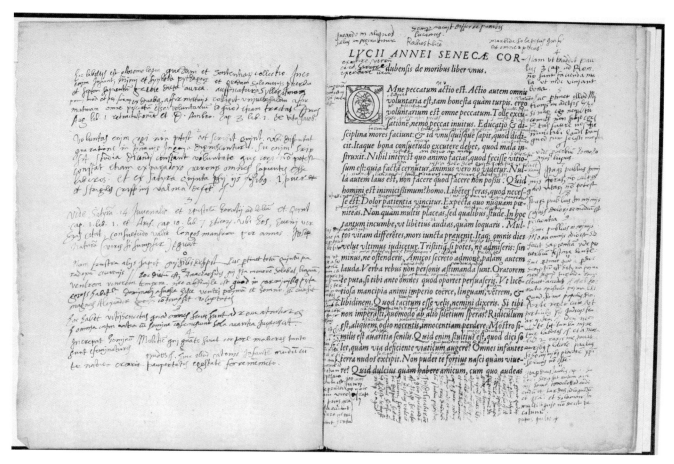

5

5 Léger Duchene
(d. 1588), ed.
L. Annei Senecae Corvbensis
De Moribvs Liber Vnus
Paris: Ex officina viduae
P. Attaingant, 1556
On Loan from a Private Collection

As is true today, early readers wrote in their books by underlining passages of interest or by adding commentary, queries, objections. The short text edited by Léger Duchene (cat. 5), made up of proverbs and maxims spuriously attributed to the Roman philosopher Seneca, was printed for use at the University of Paris. While marginalia are often a striking index of personal engagement, the manuscript annotations (ca. 1560) that fill this book and its margins are probably a student's notes on his professor's lecture, and thus point to a complex negotiation among readers experiencing and using the text collectively.

for London and England.

And ſcorne al eies, to ſée remelias eyes,
Nymphs, Euancks, ſing, for Maiors draweth nigh,
Hide me in cloſure, let him long to looke,
For were a Goddeſſe faier ti en am I.
Ile ſcale the heauens to pul her from her p'are,
   They draw the curtaines, and Muſicke plaies.
alui. Beléeue me, tho ſhe ſay that ſhe is the faireſt,
I thinke my penny ſiluer by her leaue,
   Enter raſni with his Lords in pompe, who makes a ward a-
   bout him, with him the Magi in great pompe.
raſ. Magi for loue of raſni, by your art,
By Magicke frame an arbour out of hand,
For faire remelia to diſport her in,
Meane while, I wil bethinke me on ſuch a pomp.   Exit.
The Magi with her rods beate the ground, and from vnder
   the ſame riſeth a braue arbour, the king returneth in
   another ſute while the Trumpets ſound.
raſni. Bleſt be ye man of art that grace me thus,
and bleſſed be this day where Himen hies,
To ioyne in vnion pride of heauen and earth.
   lightning and thunder wherwith remelia is ſtrooken,
What wondrous threatning noiſe is this I heare,
What flaſhing lightnings trouble our delights?
When I draw néere remelias royal tent,
I waking, dreame of ſorrow and miſhap.
   rada. Dread not O king at ordinary chance,
Theſe are but common exaltations,
Drawne from the earth, in ſubſtance hot and drie,
Or moiſt and thicke, or Meteores combuſt,
Matters and cauſes incident to time,
Enkindling in the firie Region firſt,
But, be not now a Romane Augurer,
Approach the Tent, looke on remelia.
   raſni. Thou haſt confirmd my doubts kind radagon,
Now ope ye folds where Quéne of fauour ſis,
carrying a Net within he curled locks,

         C   Within

6

The writing in multiple hands on the pages of Thomas Lodge's play (cat. 6) point even more dramatically toward a collective form of use. These marks tell us that we are looking at an early promptbook, a copy of a play used by a theater company to adapt it for use in dramatic performance. On the page shown, a passage has been cut, stage effects indicated ("musick," "thunder," "Lightening," "Arbor rises") and a stage direction added to compensate for the cut ("Ent[er] Ras[ni] Lordes & magi not paph[lagonian king])." As with the other two books in this section, use transformed this book by adapting it toward a particular end and by positioning it within a social and institutional practice.

Size

7

Size informs use, a point suggested by the two medical books shown here. Johann Wecker's tiny Latin manual (cat. 7) for the practice of general medicine is made up mainly of diagnostic guides and suggestions for the cure of specific ailments. A learned if highly compact reference book, it was designed to be carried by physicians, a function indicated both by its size and by the vellum wallet binding intended to protect the book in transit.

William Cowper's large folio anatomy (cat. 8) could not be more different, its size marking it for use within an institutional context. Designed chiefly for collective use in the anatomy theater, it offered the lecturer a set of visual aids that made vivid both the dissected body and the work of dissection. The book demonstrates an acute awareness of its size as a technology, nowhere more clearly than in table 71, which shows an anatomized, life-sized forearm emerging from a folio volume much like Cowper's own. A brilliant visual pun, the image constitutes a theoretical reflection on the use of books for representing the body. The arm and hand of the corpse are aligned with those of the anatomist and the draftsman, whose work combined to make the book possible. The image is uncanny: even as the illustration represents a dead and immobilized hand, the index finger is enlivened by a gesture of emphasis through which the book essentially points at itself.

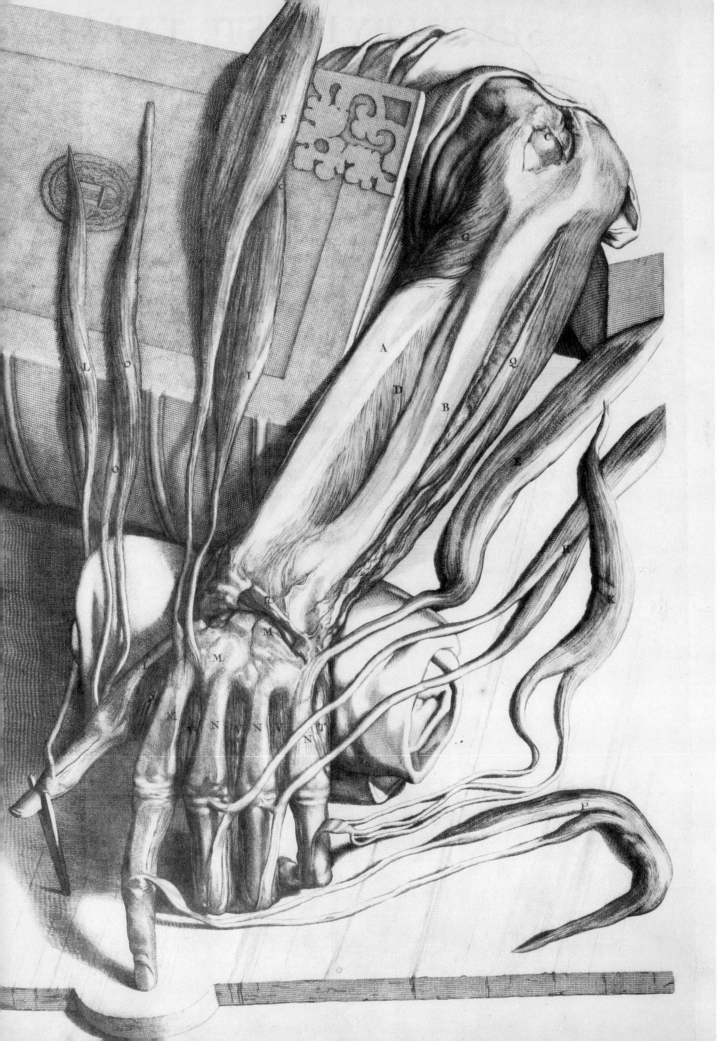

8

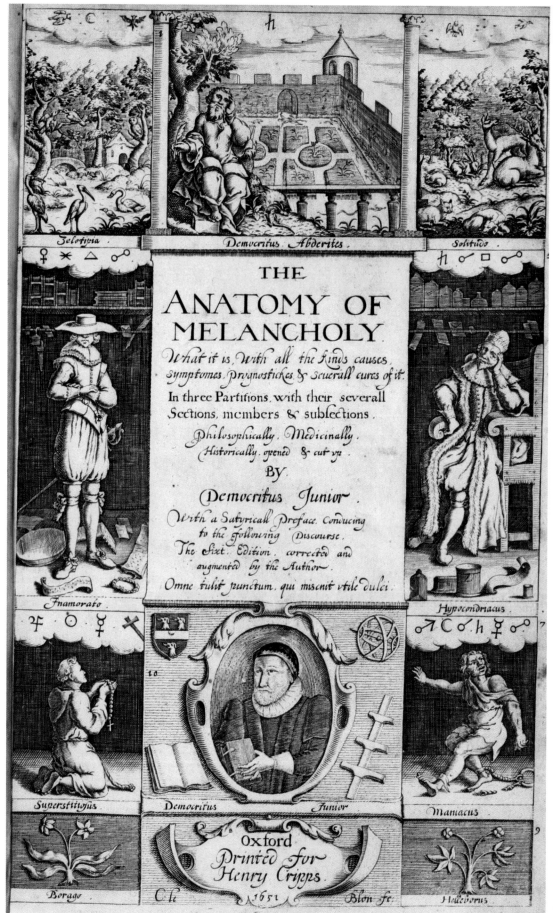

Zelotypia.

Democritus Abderites.

Solitudo.

THE

ANATOMY OF
MELANCHOLY.

What it is, With all the Kinds causes,
symptomes, Prognostickes, & seuerall cures of it.

In three Partitions, with their seuerall
Sections, members & subsections.

Philosophically, Medicinally,
Historically, opened & cut vp.

By.

Democritus Junior.

With a Satyricall Preface. Conducing
to the following Discourse.

The Sixt Edition, corrected and
augmented by the Author.

Omne tulit punctum, qui miscuit vtile dulci.

Inamorato.

Hypocondriacus.

Superstitiosus.

Democritus Junior.

Maniacus.

Borago.

Oxford
Printed for
Henry Cripps.
1651.

Blon. fe.

Helleborus.

9A

Title

9 Robert Burton
(1577–1640)
THE ANATOMY OF
MELANCHOLY.
What it is, With all the kinds causes, symptoms, prognostickes, & seuerall cures of it. In three Partitions, with their severall Sections, members & sub-sections. *Philosophically, Medicinally, Historically opened & cut vp. By Democritus Junior. With a Satyricall Preface Conducing to the following Discourse. The Sixt Edition, corrected and augmented by the Author. Omne tulit punctum. qui miscuit utile dulci.*
Oxford: Printed for
Henry Cripps, 1651
Illustrated title page, engraved by
Christoffer LeBlon
Helen and Ruth Regenstein
Collection of Rare Books

Modern transcriptions of early modern titles misrepresent them. Indeed, the standardization of spelling and typography, along with the omission of major portions of a long title, makes it harder for readers today to see that titles were a crucial dimension of the early book. Titles often guided readers by laying out the content and parts of the book and by indicating the book's value for a particular audience, field of knowledge or market sector. For reasons of space this catalog, too, uses abbreviated titles. Even here, where we have attempted to provide a more complete title of Robert Burton's encyclopedic treatise on melancholy (cat. 9), we cannot convey the visual intricacy of the original title page, with its engraved letterforms and accompanying illustrations. A further complication is that spelling in early modern books was not always consistent across multiple editions or even within a single edition. Comparing the printed half-title of this edition to its engraved title page, should we call the book an "Anatomy" or an "Anatomie"?

Burton's title (by no means the longest in the period) is in many ways typical in elaborating its subject matter and indicating the book's internal structure. By referring to the fields of philosophy, medicine and history, Burton's title designates its multiple methodological and market orientations. The illustrations on the title page are so complex as to require a commentary, called the "Argument of the Frontispiece," on the facing page. The image of Burton at the bottom center continues a tradition of author portraits from the manuscript era and works as the early modern version of a dust jacket photograph. In the highly competitive early print market, the title page was a crucial advertising strategy, a site where the author and printer could authorize the contents that followed. By means of the title, the book not only described its uses, but also reflected on itself by imagining the social and intellectual spheres to which it contributed and belonged. In this sense, it can be said that a book's theoretical dimension was produced partly by the market, even as the market was in turn refined by textual and disciplinary specialization.

9B

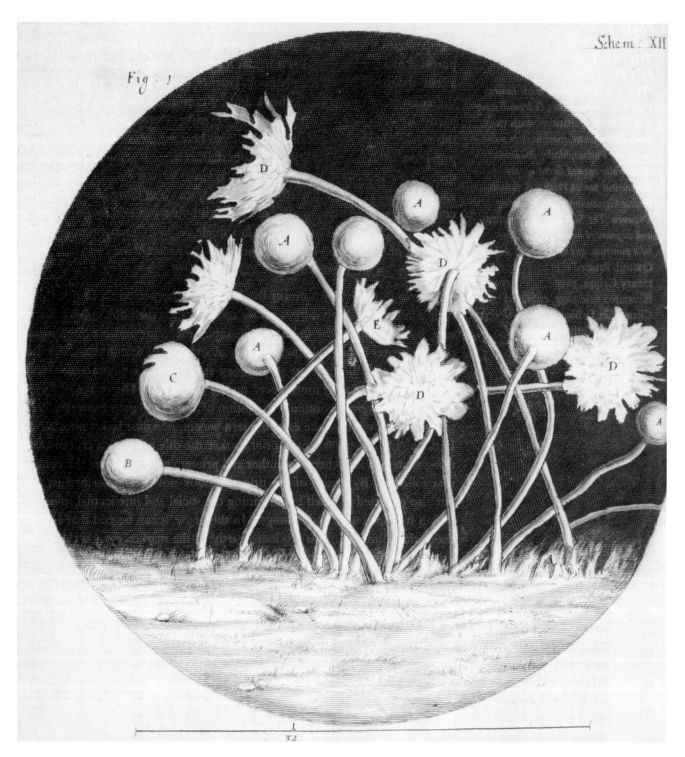

Fig: 1

Plate

10 Robert Hooke (1635–1703)
*Micrographia: Or Some Physiological
Descriptions Of Minute Bodies Made
By Magnifying Glasses*
London: by Jo. Martyn, and
Ja. Allestry, 1665
Rare Book Collection

The word "idea" comes from the Greek for "to see," and Robert Hooke's *Micrographia* (cat. 10), the first treatise to be based on the use of the microscope, redefined knowledge by redefining what it meant to see. With the use of scientific technology, to know became a matter of seeing things close up. Such technology subordinated the human eye to a new kind of vision, more specialized and hence more useful in a scientific domain.

Hooke's text offers new ways of thinking about the relationship between the printed book and the physical world. In one striking instance, he puts books themselves to a new kind of use, literally under the microscope: the mold shown in Scheme 12, he notes, was "found to bespeck & whiten over the red covers of a small book, which, it seems, were of Sheeps-skin, that being more apt to gather mould, even in a dry and clean room, then other leathers" (125).

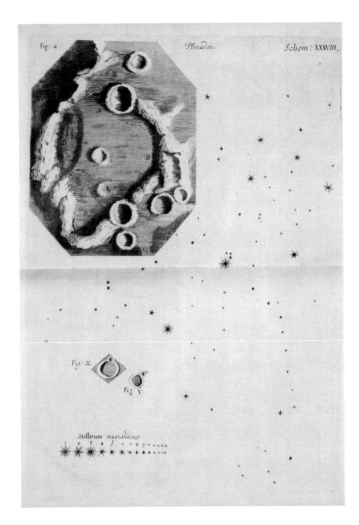

10B

Hooke magnifies the physical world external to the book, again and again drawing his readers into the domain of the material book. Although microscope technology is used throughout the book, the reader's eye is directed from narrative text to plate and back again, such that the image comes to illustrate the text and not the world. This is no less true for one of the last plates in the book, an illustration of the stars as viewed through a telescope. The microscopic and macroscopic illustrations are used here to direct the reader into the book as a substitute precisely for the scientific technologies and practices that made them possible.

As interested as *Micrographia* is in scientific accuracy, in fact, the book seems enthralled by the pleasure of its visual effects. In his description of the flea, for example, Hooke draws a distinction between the "strength and beauty of this small creature." For strength, "the *Microscope* is able to make no greater discoveries of it then the naked eye"; "But, as for the beauty of it," he says, "the *microscope* manifests it to be all over adorn'd with a curiously polish'd suit of *sable*, Armour, neatly jointed, and beset with multitudes of sharp pinns, shap'd almost like Porcupine's Quills, or bright conical Steel-bodkins" (210). The turn here to aesthetic detail and the delight of seeing the world up close suggests how book technology could forge new relationships between science and visual pleasure.

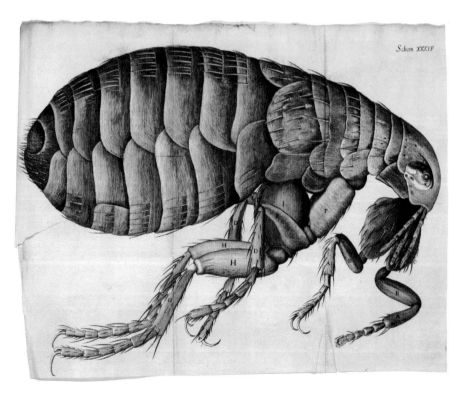

IOC

Layout

The four printed versions of the Roman Terence's plays featured here all use page layout to encourage specific kinds of reading. Many early editions of Terence, like the one published in Paris in 1552 (cat. 11), were illustrated at the start of an act or scene with images of performance, a feature that implied a theatrical space beyond the page but worked chiefly to guide the reader's eye across the page.

Humanists like Erasmus gave Terence a prominent place in the school curriculum. Schoolboys were encouraged to mine the comedies both for their moral pithiness and for the rhetorical fullness of the Latin. The three remaining Terences shown here convert the plays into a practically useful phrase book. Cornelius de Schryver's 1533 phrase book (cat. 12) abstracts Terence's plays, digesting them scene by scene into the phrases or verbal *formulae* that a schoolboy might be expected to take away from his reading and commit to memory for later use. As a pedagogical crib, it is a precursor to short-cut guides to literary texts.

11

12

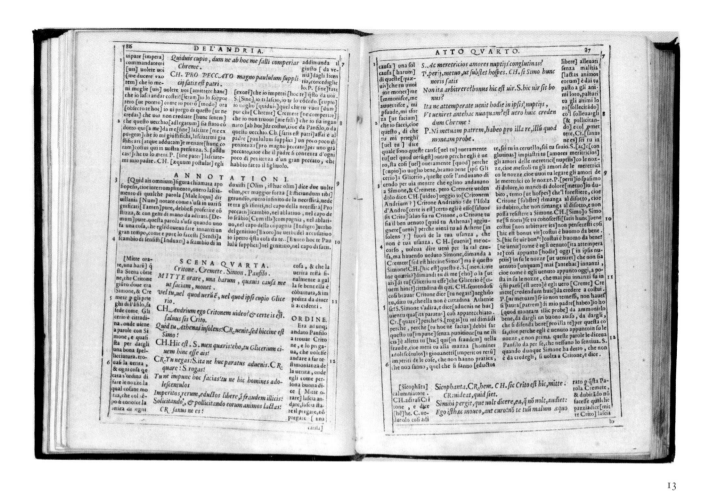

13 Giovanni Fabrini
    (1516–1580), ed.
    *Il Terentio Latino, Comentato
    In Lingua Toscana, e ridotto à la sua
    vera latinità*
    Venice: Appresso Giouambattista
    Sessa e fratelli, 1575
    Rare Book Collection

Like Schryver's book, Giovanni Fabrini's *Il Terentio Latino* (cat. 13) presents Terence as a repository of linguistic knowledge. Indeed, the book is a language textbook, designed to teach Latin to those who know Italian (*Toscano*) and Italian to those who know Latin. Adapting the layout of scholarly editions (like cat. 11) to a new end, Fabrini surrounds the Latin text not with interpretive gloss but with a word-for-word translation into the vernacular, interspersed with the Latin text, now reordered to mirror Tuscan syntax. Fabrini's ingenious page thus directs the eye according to the linguistic and textual task at hand.

14 Richard Bernard
(1568–1641), ed.
Terence in English
Cambridge: Ex Officina
Johannis Legat, 1598
Rare Book Collection

Richard Bernard's *Terence in English* (cat. 14) combines the aims of Schryver's and Fabrini's editions. Each scene is printed in Latin and then in English, and many are followed by a list of colloquial phrases to commit to memory (*formulae loquendi*). Most interestingly, these phrases are given with equally colloquial English equivalents. Like Fabrini's book, Bernard's edition thus had a double aim: while drawing attention to instances in Terence of an elegant colloquial Latin it also helped to consolidate or formalize the English vernacular.

14

The Idea of the Book

When is a book more than the sum of its parts? This section looks to theology and drama to explore the idea of "the book" as a whole. It is hard to imagine a more imposing and totalizing text than the 1611 Authorized or "King James" Bible (cat. 15). The illustrated title page emphasizes the coherence of the book and its unifying power through its many scenes of inscription, all brought

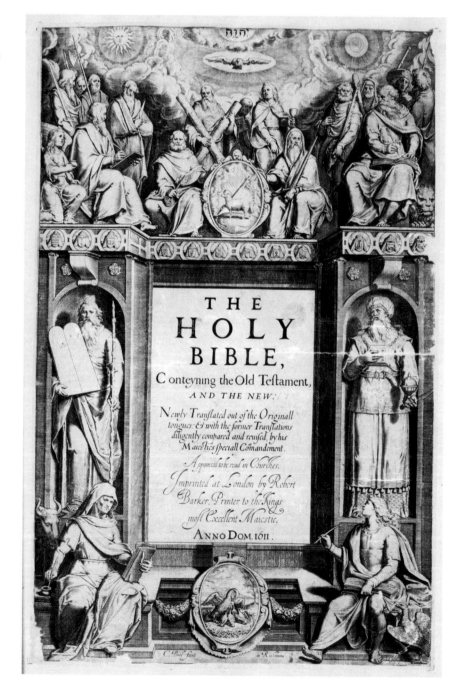

together under the sign of the ultimate author, God, as represented at the top of the page in the form of the living word or Tetragrammaton. The separate title page to the New Testament (not illustrated) offers an even more explicit fantasy of textual integrity: its decorative elements, which resemble the metal clasps on early bindings, bind together times, authors and books, integrating them, again, under the celestial inscription. The 1611 Bible was of course Protestant. The smaller Bible printed at Douai for the English Catholic community (cat. 16, not illustrated) offers a competing version, paradoxically, of the quintessential book. The difference is clear, for example, in the Douai's inclusion of II Maccabees as part of the authentic whole; the Protestant Bible appends it to the Old Testament as mere apocrypha.

The relationship between the idea of the book and secular authorship was no less complicated. In 1616 Ben Jonson famously gathered his plays, along with his poems, under the name of "Workes" (cat. 17), a word then considered more appropriate to classical authors and more serious kinds of writing. In so doing, he transformed himself from playwright to author by publicly asserting control over the dissemination of works that, as performance, were primarily understood communally. By asking that individual plays be read as part of a whole, he made available new perspectives through which to construct dramatic authorship.

17

HIDE PARKE

A
COMEDIE,

As it was presented by her Majesties Servants, at the private
house in *Drury*
Lane.

Shirley, James

Written by *James Shirly.*

LONDON,
Printed by *Tho. Cotes,* for *Andrew Crooke,*
and *William Cooke.*
1637.

18 James Shirley
    (1596–1666)
    Hide Parke A Comedie
    London: by Tho. Cotes,
    for Andrew Crooke, and
    William Cooke, 1637
    Rare Book Collection, Presented
    by the Friends of the Library

To take an example from later in the century, a Restoration reader gathered together eight separately printed plays of James Shirley in a single volume, adding a rudimentary manuscript table of contents on the front flyleaf. However modest this book may seem in comparison to Jonson's, the compiler has articulated a similar sense of the dramatist's literary authority by constituting a new whole.

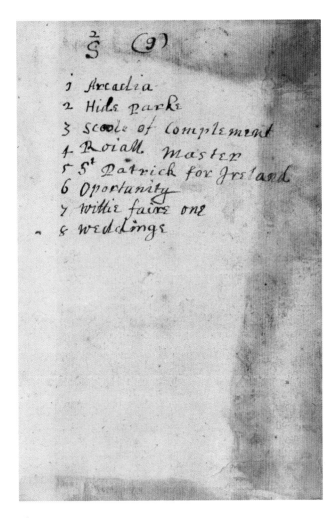

18B

Au Lecteur.

C'EST icy vn liure de bonne foy, lecteur. Il t'aduertit dés l'entrée, que ie ne m'y suis proposé aucune fin, que domestique & priuee : ie n'y ay eu nulle consideration de ton seruice, ny de ma gloire. mes forces ne sont pas capables d'vn tel dessein. Ie l'ay voué à la commodité particuliere de mes parens & amis : à ce que m'ayant perdu (ce qu'ils ont à faire bien tost) ils y puissent retrouuer aucuns traits de mes conditions & humeurs, & que par ce moyen ils nourrissent plus entiere & plus vfue, la connoissance qu'ils ont eu de moy. Si c'eust esté pour rechercher la faueur du monde : ie me fusse paré de beautez empruntées, ou me fusse tendu & bãdé en ma meilleure démarche. Ie veus qu'õ m'y voie en ma façõ simple, naturelle & ordinaire, sans estude & artifice : car c'est moy que ie peins. Mes defauts s'y liront au vif. mes imperfections & ma forme naïfue, autant que la reuerence publique me l'a permis. Que si i'eusse esté parmy ces nations qu'on dict viure encore sous la douce liberté des premieres loix de nature, ie t'assure que ie m'y fusse tres volontiers peint tout entier, & tout nud. Ainsi, lecteur, ie suis moy-mesmes la matiere de mon liure : ce n'est pas raison que tu employes ton loisir en vn subiect si friuole & si vain. A Dieu donq, de Montaigne, ce 12. Iuin. 1588.

ã ij

PART II

Parts and Wholes: From Matter to Method

"PARTS AND WHOLES" explores the ways in which books were partitioned through elements such as prefaces, tables of contents, indexes and diagrammatic schemes that visually represented the organization of textual material. These tools suggested an order among parts and helped readers navigate the book and orient themselves in relation to it. At the same time, they offered an abstract of the book and even a model for processing information. "Analysis," a dividing of a whole into parts, is at once a form of cognition and of textual organization. Even a simple index, for example, by breaking a book into what it takes to be its most significant parts, constitutes an interpretation of the whole. And a table of contents can be both a guide to use and a theorization of the contents.

Dividing a book into parts is always a form of thinking. This is clearly exemplified in the early modern tradition of commonplacing, a method of making books one's own by breaking them down into, and digesting, their most significant (i.e. usable) parts. The process of thinking in and through parts, so integral to commmonplacing, is related to forms of cognition and textual organization that relied on the isolated and particular case. By making the single case representative, disciplines such as law, theology and history could identify general theoretical principles and even imply a system of knowledge underlying the case. Case thinking demands the reader's participation in the methodical constitution of general knowledge. Books organized as collections of cases offer a material record of the complexities involved in thinking from particular to general as from part to whole.

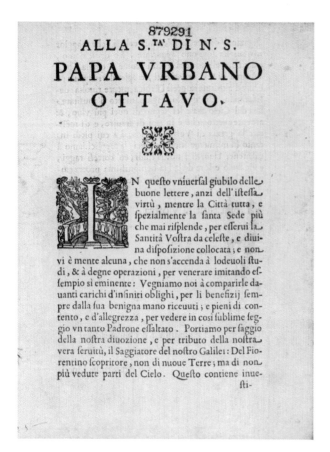

19A   19B

19   Galileo Galilei
(1564–1642)
Il saggiatore
Rome: Appresso Giacomo
Mascardi, 1623
Rare Book Collection, Formerly
in the Collection of Herbert
McLean Evans

Prefaces and errata sheets help us think about book use because they establish particular relationships between author and reader. Like the titles, prefaces to the general reader or to a specific patron guided use by highlighting or theorizing the social significance and methodological stakes of the topic. Furthermore, they offered the opportunity for presenting a version of the reader to himself or herself, as a patron worthy to be flattered, or as one of those capable of being educated.

The two prefaces in this section offer particularly complex instances of the author-reader relationship. The dedication in Galileo Galilei's *Il saggiatore* (cat. 19) to the newly named Pope Urban VIII functioned as a quasi-imprimatur, not unlike the official permission to print that appears on the opposite page. Interestingly, however, it was Galileo's friends at the Lincean academy in Florence who composed the preface and recommended its inclusion. At the same time that this distanced the author from the direct promotion of his book, it offered a second, collective sanction to mirror the implicit or hoped-for sanction of the pope.

AN ADVERTISEMENT TO
the Reader.

Hough I purpofed not to fpeake any thing to the Reader, otherwife then by way of Epilogue in the end of the Booke, both becaufe I efteemed that to be the fitteft place, to giue my Reafons, why I refpited the handling of the two laft Chapters, till another time, and alfo, becaufe I thought not that any man might well and properly be called a Reader, till he were come to the end of the Booke: yet, becaufe both he, and I, may fuffer fome difaduantages, if he fhould not be fore-poffeffed, and warned in fome things, I haue changed my purpofe in that point.

For his owne good therefore (in which I am alfo intereffed) I muft firft intreat him, that he will be pleafed, before hee reade, to amend with his pen, fome of the moft important errors, which are hereafter noted to haue paffed in the printing. Becaufe in the Reading, he will not perchance fufpect nor fpy them, and fo he may runne a danger, of being either deceiued, or fcandalized.

20

20 John Donne
(1572–1631)
Pseudomartyr
London: by W. Stansby for
Walter Burre, 1610
Helen and Ruth Regenstein
Collection of Rare Books

Addressing a reader in a preface did not necessarily mean that the reader ever read it or the book. In the ingenious preface or "Advertisement" to the reader of his *Pseudomartyr* (cat. 20), John Donne plays on this point in order to establish an alternative authority for the reader, one that emerges only through an actual engagement with the book. Writing that he would have preferred to address the reader "by way of Epilogue in the end of the Booke," Donne explains that "I thought not that any man might well and properly be called a Reader, till he were come to the end of the Booke."

Errata sheets also functioned to establish the book's authority by implying a process of scrupulous proofreading in the final stages of producing the material book. Nearly always, the errata sheet directs the reader, not only to make the noted corrections, but also to become a scrupulous reader by making further corrections, as required, on his or her own. The errata sheet at the end of the Herbert M. Evans copy of *Il saggiatore* is unusually interesting in that Galileo himself has added, in his own hand, a correction missing on the errata sheet itself. At this moment, he is at once scrupulous author and scrupulous reader.

Index

The index (from the Latin for "forefinger" and "point out") became instrumental to the use of the book, not only by making the contents usefully accessible but also by identifying what were, at least in theory, the book's central subjects. Indexes allowed for non-sequential reading and for accessing information in ways other than those suggested by the book's narrative logic. In fact, it was possible to read an index first, or even instead of the book. Something like this happened in the case of *Histrio-mastix* (cat. 21), a massive anti-theatrical treatise by the Puritan polemicist William Prynne. An entry in the concluding index or "table" cost Prynne his ears. Under the heading "*Women-Actors*" Prynne had directed his readers first to "notorious whores. p. 162, 214, 215, 1002, 1003." This entry was taken by King Charles to be an insult against the Queen, Henrietta Maria, who took speaking parts in plays presented at court.

Prynne's fate dramatically shows that indexes are not neutral. This is no less true of the index that concludes *The Temple*, George Herbert's posthumously published collection of poems (cat. 22). This was the first such index to an English book of poems. Although it does nothing more than list the titles of the individual poems in alphabetical order, it was innovative in thus making the book available for a specific, devotional use. A reader, that is, could use the

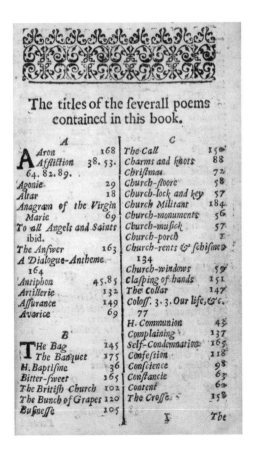

22

65

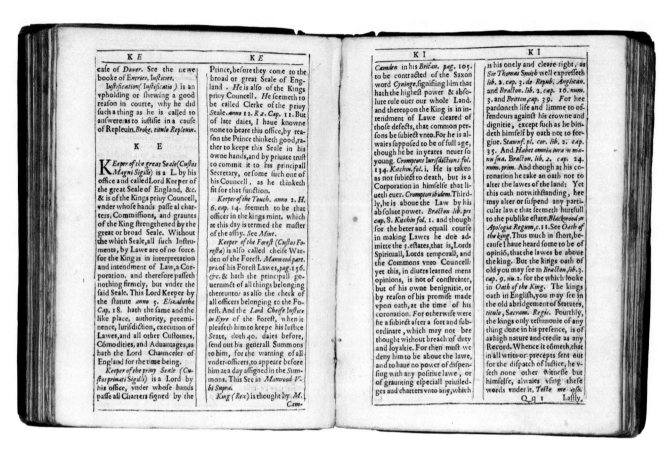

23

index to find poems on a given religious topic appropriate for meditation: "Avarice," "Self-Condemnation," "Conscience," "The Crosse," "Easter," "Love," "Mortification," "Sunday," "Ungratefulnesse."

Some books, of course, *are* indexes. Dictionaries too are always interpretive, working as they do to constitute (and not simply describe) a field of learning or language use. John Cowell's *The Interpreter* (cat. 23), intended as a comprehensive alphabetical guide to the terms of English common law, was burned by royal proclamation for subversively taking up constitutional questions in such entries as "king," "prerogative," "parliament" and "subsidy." Cowell's entries, which invariably promoted the absolute authority of the king, angered members of parliament as being prejudicial to their rights. In the proclamation against the book, however, King James defined Cowell's impudence in different terms, saying that the arbitrary alphabetic form of his book had "placed all kinds of purposes belonging to Government and Monarchie in his way." Cowell's error, in this formulation, was in choosing an indexical form that allowed or required him to list and define matters that, according to the king, were beyond the scope of a subject's natural authority. Cowell's dictionary shows how, in making a field navigable and usable, an index may not only define the limits of that field but also constitute itself as an authority on it.

Diagram

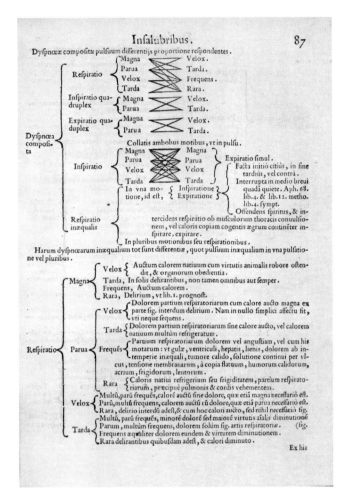

24

Graphic elements such as diagrams and tables of contents were guides both to using and to thinking about the book. The visual aids highlighted here organize medical, legal, literary and musical information, transforming narratives apprehended in time into condensed graphic forms comprehended in space. These abstractions of subject matter are closely associated with the pedagogical innovations of Pierre de la Ramée (Petrus Ramus, 1515–1572), a philosopher and noted teacher who aimed to update Aristotelian method, partly through the use of such schematic (and, it was sometimes said, reductive) models of thought.

The table that Jacques Dubois (Jacobus Sylvius) included in his medical textbook (cat. 24) helps a doctor keep in mind a set of possible relationships between breathing and pulse and make different diagnostic inferences based on them. The table is thus both a practical aid and a guide to methodical analysis.

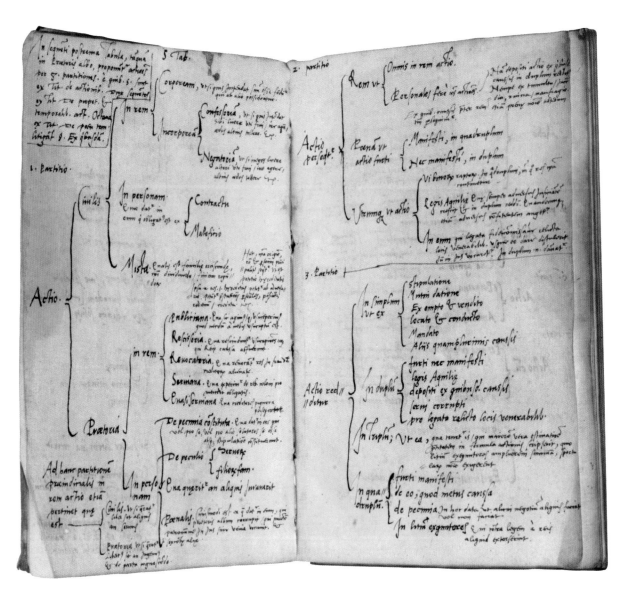

25 Conrad Lagus
(d. 1546)
Methodica Ivris Vtriusqve Traditio
Lyon: Apud Seb. Gryphivm, 1544
Rare Book Collection

Conrad Lagus's textbook on civil law (cat. 25) has no such diagram. An early reader, however, responding to the Ramist phenomenon, has composed a table of his own on four blank leaves at the front of the book. The pages show the reader's methodical digestion of Lagus's narrative elaboration of distinct kinds of legal action.

Abraham Fraunce's *Lawiers Logike* (cat. 26) was designed to foster methodical thinking among English common lawyers by exposing the logical structure inhering in their legal texts and mode of analysis. Fraunce takes his examples from two principal sources, one poetic and one legal: Edmund Spenser's 1579 *Shepheardes Calendar* and Edmund Plowden's 1571 *Comentaries*, a collection of reports on recent legal cases (see cat. 33). An example of early literary analysis,

26 Abraham Fraunce
    (1587–1633)
    *The Lawiers Logike, exemplifying the
    præcepts of Logike by the practise of
    the common Lawe*
    London: by William How, for
    Thomas Gubbin, and
    T. Newman, 1588
    Rare Book Collection

27 Georg Fabricius
    (1589–1645)
    *Thesaurus Philosophicus Sive
    Tabulae Totius Philosophiae*
    Braunsweig: Typis et sumptibus
    Andreae Dunckeri, 1624
    Rare Book Collection,
    Richard P. McKeon Collection

the table shown here reduces one of Virgil's eclogues to a set of spatial dichotomies in order to show its logical structure. Fraunce's striking alignment of poetry and law emerges in part through the extraordinary portability of the Ramist diagram, its ability to order very diverse kinds of material.

In contrast to these tables, Georg Fabricius's dichotomy of musical harmonies (cat. 27) seems, for all its beauty, so elementary as to be of little intellectual use. But the table also demonstrates how even a reductive schematic organization might be pedagogically useful precisely in putting fundamental distinctions in front of a reader.

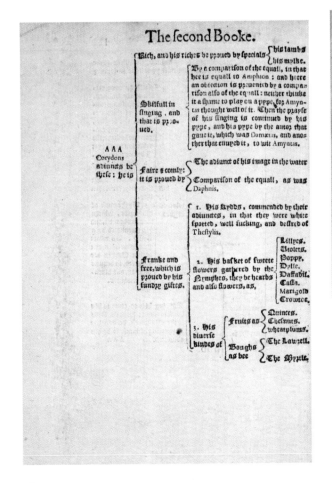

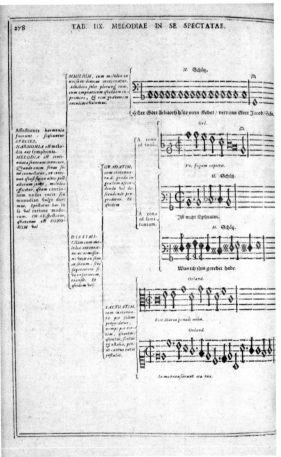

26

27

Commonplace Thinking

28 Thomas Ducke (fl. 1619) and
   Edward Jones (fl. 1686)
   Commonplace Book
   Manuscript, compiled ca. 1619
   and 1686
   Codex Manuscript Collection

A commonplace book is at once a book form and a method of reading. Commonplacing was a system of using books in which readers digested them by extracting, ordering and recording particular phrases or passages in notebooks of their own. This process encouraged readers to atomize books by isolating units that might later be useful in another context. While the commonplace book allowed readers to personalize their reading by making it useful, this process of textual engagement was also highly prescribed, "common" in the sense that it filtered one's reading through social norms that determined which textual elements were significant and which were not.

The early pages of Thomas Ducke's ca. 1619 commonplace book (cat. 28) digested material under general headings corresponding to the order of the Christian universe (God, Christ, Law, Heaven, etc.). His interests, however, go beyond the theological to include, for example, a long list of amusing stories, presumably compiled for his pleasure or to help him remember them for later

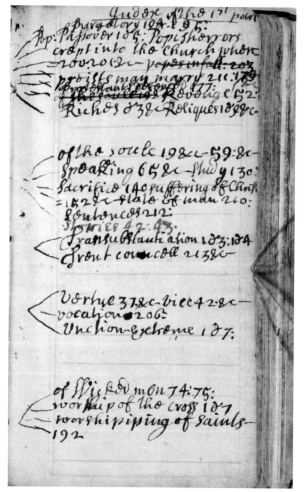

28

29

use at the dinner table. By their nature, manuscript commonplace books such as Ducke's would seem to be most useful to their compiler. This was not always the case. An interesting feature of the book is that it was used by a second reader around 1686, one Edward Jones, who supplemented it by adding stories and jokes, mainly of a sexual nature. Most remarkably, he added an index to the pages compiled by Ducke sixty years earlier. Jones's appropriation of Ducke's book can be seen as a logical step in a process in which all reading was appropriation.

The small early seventeenth-century legal commonplace book (cat. 29) was probably compiled by a law student at the Inns of Court in London. Although it had a specific professional function, the book can also be seen as a personal document in the way Ducke's more wide-ranging book is, since it was through such books that lawyers made a disciplinary structure their own. Drawing both *selfe respectable by vertue and sufficiency, and amiable by his goodnesse, and gentlenesse of maners.* The very cinders of so rich a matter, have their value : so have the bones and reliques of honourable men, whom we hold in respect and reverence. No age can be so crazed and drooping in a man that hath lived honourably, but must needes prove venerable, and especially vnto his children, whose mindes ought so to be directed by the parents, that reason and wisedome, not necessity and neede, nor rudenesse and compulsion, may make them know and performe their duty.

> —— *& errat longè, mea quidem sententia,*
> *Qui imperium credat esse gravius aut stabilius,*
> *Vi quod fit, quàm illud quod amicitia adiungitur.*
> In mine opinion he doth much mistake,
> Who, that command more graue, more firme doth take,
> Which force doth get, then that which friendships make.

Ter. Adelph. act. 1. sce. 1, 39

I vtterly condemne all maner of violence in the education of a yong spirit, brought vp to honour and liberty. There is a kinde of slavishnesse in churlish-rigor, and servility in compulsion ; and I hold, that *that which can not be compassed by reason, wisedome and discretion, can never be attained by force and constraint.* So was I brought vp : they tell mee, that in all my youth, I never felt rod but twice, and that very lightly. And what education I have had my selfe, the same have I given my children. But such is my ill hap, that they die all very yong : yet hath *Leonora* my onely daughter escaped this misfortune, and attained to the age of six yeares, and somewhat more : for the conduct of whose youth, and punishment of hir childish faults (the indulgence of hir mother applying it selfe very mildely vnto it) was never other meanes vsed but gentle words. And were my desire frustrate, there are diverse other causes to take hold-of, without reproving my discipline, which I know to be just and naturall. I would also have beene much more religious in that towards male-children, not borne to serve as women, and of a freer condition. I should have loved to have stored their minde with ingenuity and liberty. I have seene no other effects in rods, but to make childrens mindes more remisse, or more maliciously head-strong. Desire we to be loved of our children? Will we remove all occasions from them to wish our death ? (although no occasion of so horrible and vnnaturall wishes, can either be just or excusable) *nullum scelus rationem habet,* no ill deede hath a good reason.

Let vs reasonably accommodate their life, with such things as are in our power. And therfore should not we marry so yoong, that our age doe in a maner confound it selfe with theirs. For, this inconvenience doth vnavoidably cast vs into many difficulties, and encombrances. This I speake, chiefly vnto Nobility, which is of an idle disposition, or loitering condition, and which (as we say) liveth onely by hir lands or rents : for else, where life standeth vpon gaine ; plurality and company of children is an easefull furtherance of busbandry. They are as many new implements to thrive, and instruments to grow rich. I was married at thirty yeeres of age, and commend the opinion of thirty-five, which is said to be *Aristotles.* Plato would have no man married before thirty, and hath good reason to scoffe at them that will defer it till after fifty-five, and then marry ; and condemneth their breed as vnworthy of life and sustenance. *Thales* appointed the best limites, who by his mother, being instantly vrged to marry whilest he was yong, answered that it was not yet time ; and when he came to be old he said it was no more time. A man must refuse opportunity to every importunate action. The ancient *Gaules* deemed it a shamefull reproach, to have the acquaintance of a woman before the age of twenty yeares ; and did especially recommend vnto men that sought to be trained vp in warres, the carefull preseruation of their maiden-head, vntill they were of good yeeres, forsomuch as by loosing it in youth, courages are thereby much weakened and greatly empaired, and by copulation with women, diverted from all vertuous action.

> *Ma hor coginnto à gio vinetta sposa,*
> *Listo homai de' figli' era invilito*
> *Ne gli affetti di padre & di marito.*
> But now conjoyn'd to a fresh-springing spouse,
> Ioy'd in his children, he was thought-abased,
> In passions twixt a Sire, and husband placed.

Mulcasses King of *Thunes*, he whom the Emperour *Charles* the fifth restored vnto his

owne

30 Michel de Montaigne
(1533–1592)
Essais
Paris: Chez Abel L'Angelier, 1588
Rare Book Collection,
Bequest of Lillian A. Wells

31 Michel de Montaigne
Essayes Written In French By
Michael Lord of Montaigne. . .
Done Into English according to the
last French edition, by Iohn Florio
London: by Melch. Bradwood
for Edward Blount and
William Barret, 1613
On Loan From a
Private Collection

on written texts and on oral sources, including legal decisions in the courts and exercises central to legal training, lawyers used commonplacing to synthesize information, thereby helping to constitute the law as a field of textual practice.

Michel de Montaigne's *Essais* (cat. 30, see detail p. 60) famously began as his commonplace book. The topical structure of the book and the individual essays ("De l'amitié," "Des Cannibales," "Du dormir") mirrors the commonplace organization of material. In a nice reversal of the process whereby Montaigne made his book, an early English reader of John Florio's translation of Montaigne (cat. 31) seems to have digested the essays according to topics of his own. His annotations variously underscore Montaigne's text, as on page 215, with his emphatic "mark this" and his approving "a fittinge age to mayrye." Most interestingly, he makes Montaigne's generic description of a military hero historical and local, by identifying the type with the German "Count Mannsfield," a leader whose visits to London in 1624 consolidated his English reputation for heroism. Sometimes the reader follows Montaigne's categories, sometimes not. On page 41, next to a famous anecdote about a woman who turned into a man by jumping over a fence, the English reader has written "for wenches lepeing [leaping]." Has he imagined this improbable heading as a category of use or thought?

The first Booke. 41

of *Soiffons* had in confirmation, named *Germane*, and all the inhabitants there about have
both knowne and feene to be a woman-childe, vntill fhe was two and twentie yeares of
age, called by the name of *Marie*. He was, when I faw him, of good yeares, and had a long
beard, and was yet vnmarried. He faith, that vpon a time leaping, and ftraining himfelfe
to overleape an other, he wot not how, but where before he was a woman, he fuddenly felt
the inftrument of a man to come out of him; and to this day the maidens of that towne

for wenche lepem

31B

73

The burning of Iohn Kurde Martyr, at
Northampton.

The martyrdō
of Iohn Kurde
at Northamp-
ton.an.1557.
Septemb.20.

The martyrdō
of Iohn Kurde
at Northamp-
ton.an.1557.
Septemb.20.

32A

The cruell burning of Robert Samuel, martyr.

The martyr-
Dome of Rob.
Samuel bur-
ned at Ipſwich.
An 1555.
Auguſt. 31.

The martyr-
Dome of Rob.
Samuel bur-
ned at Ipſwich.
An 1555.
Auguſt. 31.

32B

The martyrdome of Thomas Iueſon.

The martyr-
Dome of Tho-
mas Iueſon,at
Chicheſter.An.
1555.Iuly.

The martyr-
Dome of Tho-
mas Iueſon,at
Chicheſter.An.
1555.Iuly.

32C

Case Thinking

32 John Foxe
(1516–1587)
The seconde Volume Of
The Ecclesiasticall Historie,
conteyning The Acts And
Monvments of Martyrs
London: by Peter Short, 1597
Rare Book Collection

How does one move methodically from part to whole, from the particular to the general? An individual case can exemplify a general rule or provide an exception to it; similar cases might be connected together through analogy in order to generalize from them. Because it emerges from circumstance and situation, "case thinking" is based in a specificity that can seem antithetical to method itself. As a result, textual strategies for dealing with the particular instance become unusually important for the constitution of method.

John Foxe's vast ecclesiastical history (cat. 32) catalogs case after case of individuals martyred for the Protestant faith. Repetition is of the essence, since it is through repetition that martyrdom, as a form of subjection, could come to constitute national history. Although the individual case must have priority in the kind of story Foxe wants to tell, not least because of how he means to affect the reader, it is also true that the logic of accumulation and repetition diminished the distinctions among cases. The individual case is a form and formula; it is for this reason that the same illustration can usefully function in the book on pages 1528, 1547 and 1833 to represent three separate martyrs. The use of this woodcut speaks to the fact that illustrations in early modern books could work simply to organize textual material on the page and to offer a symbolic or indexical cue to a topic. In Foxe's book, however, the repeated illustrations speak also to the tension between case and method in the making of history.

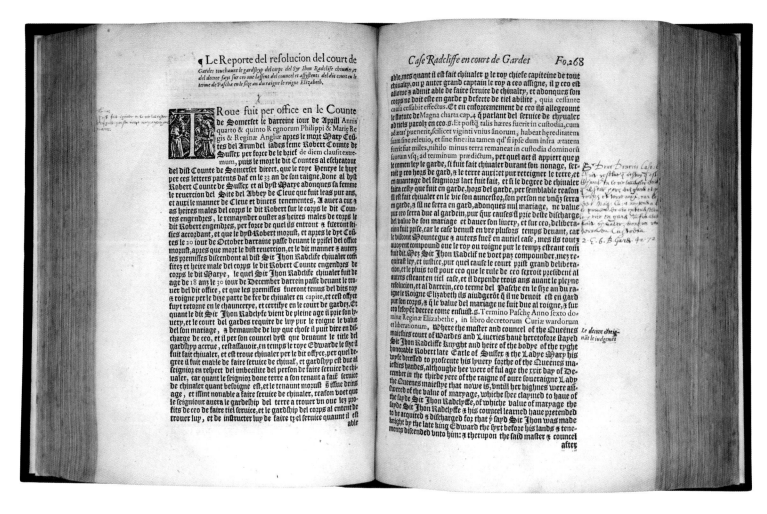

33

33 Edmund Plowden
(1518–1585)
*Les Comentaries, ou les
Reportes de Edmunde Plowden*
[London]: In ædibus Richardi
Tottelli, [1571]–1579
Rare Book Collection,
Ruben T. Durrett Collection

English lawyers thought about their practice in terms of particular legal cases, going to them both to learn the skills of pleading that were required in the courtroom and, increasingly, to extract from them the principles of the unwritten law. Edmund Plowden's collected reports of individual law cases (cat. 33) was the first to print only those in which general legal principles had been explicitly stated and could be abstracted as such (and so written into commonplace books like cat. 29). In so doing, Plowden provided an important model for reporting the legal case in terms of generalizable law, a textual development that allowed precedent (or "case thinking" in the modern sense) to emerge as the dominant structure of English legal thought.

34 Thomas Ashe
(fl. 1600–1618), ed.
*Abridgement des touts
les Cases Reportes alarge per
Mounsieur Plowden*
London: for the Company of
Stationers, 1607
On Loan From a
Private Collection

Legal abridgments like Thomas Ashe's condensed version of Plowden (cat. 34) helped lawyers avoid in another way the difficulties of sifting through innumerable particulars in their practical and case-by-case pursuit of method. Early readers of both Ashe and Plowden have left marginalia, the traces of their part in completing the books by synthesizing and generalizing from their particulars. The blank space of the margin here is critical matter for methodical work.

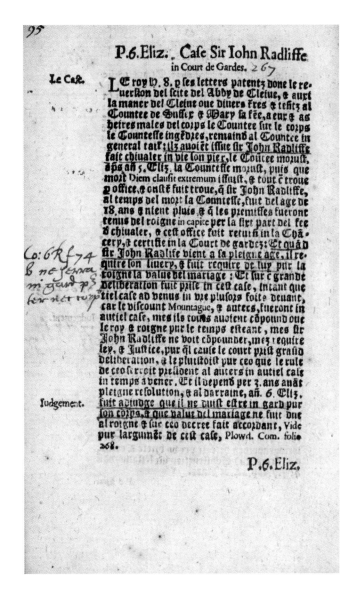

PART III

The How-to Book

NO LITERARY GENRE promotes its utility as explicitly as the "how-to" book. Although instructional manuals written for a wide range of specialized groups existed prior to the advent of print, the unprecedented scale of reproduction and dissemination that print enabled effectively transformed the how-to book into a new genre. As an instructional guide adaptable to all spheres of public and private life, the how-to book taught skills integral to fields like theology, medicine, the mechanical arts and domestic husbandry. Also, more generally, it introduced readers to rhetorical practice, to social and ethical forms of conduct, and to the cultivation of personhood itself.

Such books are, on the one hand, clearly didactic, grounding their authority in the expertise of the author. On the other, they enabled the reader to assume new forms of authority (it is no coincidence that self-help books are so often written in vernacular languages). By positioning readers as actors, by requiring them to actualize knowledge by performing it, these books promised a transformation of identity. Rather than being at the margin of the genre, therefore, conduct and psychological self-help books were arguably at its center, since they made so explicit the idea of self-making that underwrote even the more narrowly instrumental how-to books.

It is important to remember that how-to books were oriented toward fields of knowledge still in formation. As such, they required readers to think imaginatively and speculatively. Even as they fitted their readers into this or that prescribed identity, they also offered them a glimpse beyond the horizon of prescriptive knowledge, insisting as they did on the reader's participation, and on the logical priority of his or her experience. The how-to book gives experience form. In this sense, Baconian empiricism (which so disrupted the grounds of earlier scientific authority) can be seen as the genre's logical extension, yoking together as it does experience and experiment, transforming the practice of the one into the method of the other.

35 Thomas Wilson
(1525?–1581)
*The Arte of Rhetorike, for the vse of
all suche as are studious of Eloquence*
London: by Ihon Kingston, 1567
Rare Book Collection
Not illustrated

Rhetoric is a practical art, prescribing the use of language and gesture for particular situations and particular ends. In that sense, the four books brought together here can be thought of as how-to books for self-expression at the border between public and private. Like Thomas Wilson's *Arte of Rhetorike*, a vernacular guide to classical oratorical practice (cat. 35, not illustrated), John Bulwer's *Chirologia* (cat. 36) is a *manual* of expression, in this case a handbook about the hand itself. Although it looks forward to sign language in our sense

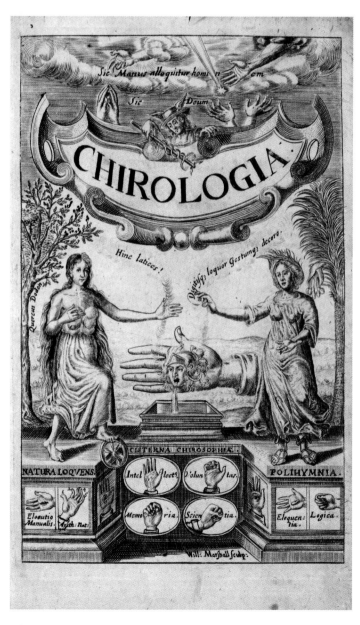

36A

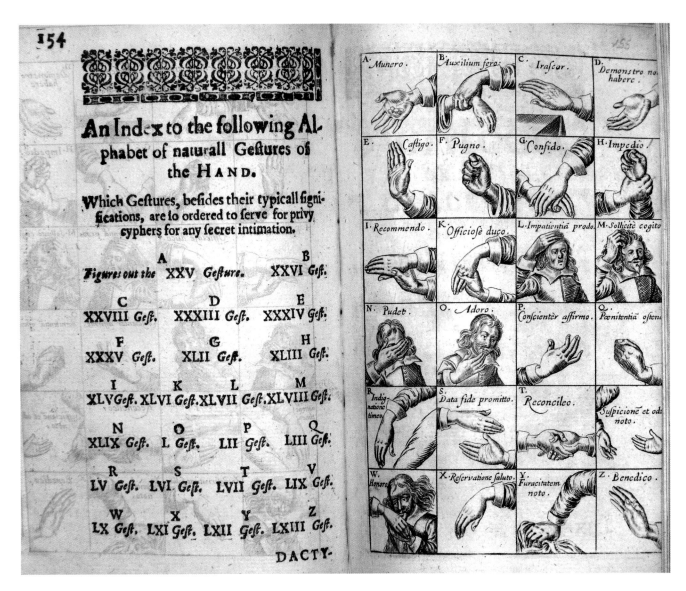

An Index to the following Alphabet of naturall Gestures of the HAND.

Which Gestures, besides their typicall significations, are so ordered to serve for privy cyphers for any secret intimation.

	A		B
Figures out the	XXV Gesture.		XXVI Gest.
C	D		E
XXVIII Gest.	XXXIII Gest.		XXXIV Gest.
F	G		H
XXXV Gest.	XLII Gest.		XLIII Gest.
I	K	L	M
XLV Gest.	XLVI Gest.	XLVII Gest.	XLVIII Gest.
N	O	P	Q
XLIX Gest.	L Gest.	LII Gest.	LIII Gest.
R	S	T	V
LV Gest.	LVI Gest.	LVII Gest.	LIX Gest.
W	X	Y	Z
LX Gest.	LXI Gest.	LXII Gest.	LXIII Gest.

DACTY-

36B

36 John Bulwer
(fl. 1648–1654)
Chirologia: Or The Natvrall Langvage Of The Hand
London: by Tho. Harper, 1644
Rare Book Collection

of the phrase, it is more accurately described as a guide to manual gesture, illustrating and cataloging the "natural" logic of bodily expression. At the same time, the book offers itself up for an alternative form of use as a system of cryptography, in that the same gestures can "serve for privy ciphers for any secret intimation." The very gestures that Bulwer insisted were universal and "naturall" were also available, that is, for the construction of covert, private communication.

37

37 Ambrosio de Salazar
(b. 1575?)
Iardin de Flores Santas
Paris: En la tienda de
G. Robinot, 1616
Rare Book Collection

38 *The Booke of Common Prayer*
London: by Robert Barker, 1606
Rare Book Collection, Gift of
Mrs. George Langhorne
Not illustrated

Prayer can be experienced as one of the most intimate and immediate forms of self-expression. And yet, publicly or privately, talking with God is also a rhetorical art. A tiny devotional intended for the most intimate use, Ambrosio de Salazar's *Iardin de Flores Santas* (*Garden of Holy Flowers*, cat. 37) prescribes times and forms of prayer by which a conventional language (like that of the penitential psalms) could be internalized and naturalized as one's own. Like Salazar's devotional, *The Booke of Common Prayer* (cat. 38, not illustrated) is at once public and private. As the official prayer book for a newly national church, it gave to English Protestantism the language and rhetoric in which public prayers and rituals were to be conducted. In this sense, individual members of the congregation were subjected to authorized forms of expression and so instituted as members of the English church. These how-to books for the arts of expression not only taught readers to speak but also guided them toward complex communal identities.

39 Hannah Woolley
(fl. 1670)
The Queene-like Closet, Or Rich Cabinet: Stored with all manner of Rare Receipts for Preseruing, Candying and Cookery
London: for Richard Lowndes, 1672
John Crerar Collection of Rare Books in the History of Science and Medicine

Books that instructed readers how to do specific tasks in professional or domestic life can seem straightforward, but they are often dense with implication for the relations between persons and practices and practices and professions. The recipes, for example, in Hannah Woolley's cookbook (cat. 39) depended upon social and economic norms that the book was partly responsible for creating.

39

40 Anonymous
De Sectione mensaria
[n.p.: n.p., 16—?]
John Crerar Collection of
Rare Books in the History of
Science and Medicine

To use the book was to educate oneself in dietary norms and in culinary forms of social self-fashioning. Similarly, *De Sectione mensaria* (*On Carving at Table*, cat. 40), an anonymous and undated French carving book, guided the user in carving techniques for various kinds of meat and fish, as well as in ornamental food presentation, illustrating, for example, how to cut and serve a lemon in the shape of an insect, turtle, heart or rose. Despite its Latin title, the book is in French, designed specifically for travelers to other countries as a guide to the performance of this particular form of civility. An early modern version of Martha Stewart's *Living*, the book teaches aesthetic appreciation and social affiliation through food preparation, working simultaneously as a how-to-do and a how-to-be book.

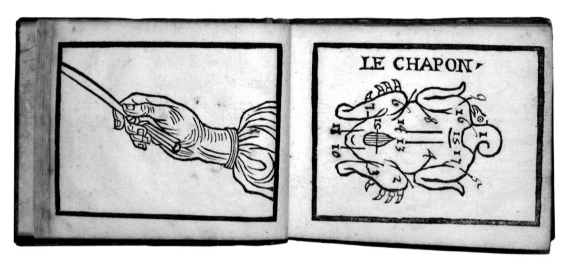

40A

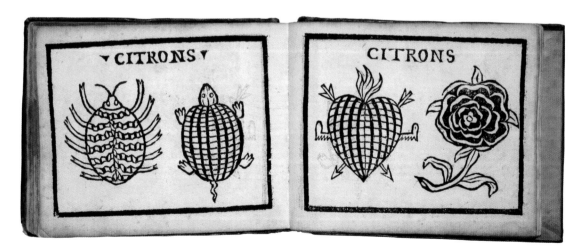

40B

41 Peter Lowe
(ca. 1550–ca. 1612)
*A Discourse of the Whole Art
of Chyrvrgerie*
London: by Thomas Purfoot, 1612
Rare Book Collection,
Morris Fishbein Collection

42 Joseph Moxon
(1627–1700)
*Mechanick Exercises: Or The
Doctrine of Handy-Works. Applied
to the Art of Tvrning*
London: for Joseph Moxon, 1680
Rare Book Collection

43 William Leybourn
(1626–1716)
*The Compleat Surveyor, Containing
the whole Art of Surveying of Land.*
London: by R. and W. Leybourn,
for G. Sawbridge, 1657
2nd ed., with many additions
John Crerar Collection of
Rare Books in the History of
Science and Medicine
Not illustrated

Portraiture of a drie suture.

41

The remaining three books in this section are concerned with emergent professional fields and identities: Peter Lowe's surgeon (cat. 41), Joseph Moxon's skilled craftsman (cat. 42, see detail p. x) and William Leybourn's surveyor (cat. 43, not illustrated). Because these professions were still in formation, each of the books was useful in two ways, instructing individual practitioners and consolidating the claims of the group as a whole to a field of knowledge or expertise. In other words, at the same time that the books offered general instruction on the practice of an "Art," they laid the groundwork for a series of specialized professional identities capable of defining the theoretical nature of their expertise. In this respect, it is notable that the three titles imply or "invent" a field by highlighting the relationship between practice and "Doctrine," between a specific "Art" and its totalized "Whole."

YOUTH

RECREATION

DISPOSITION.

ACQVAINTANCE

EDVCATION

MODERATION

VOCATION

PERFECTION

The English Gentleman

SPES IN CÆLIS

PES IN TERRIS.

Ro: Vaughan fecit

How to Be Somebody

The Renaissance conduct manual was a how-to book designed explicitly for the performance of personhood, in terms of categories such as gender, rank, age or national and regional affiliation. To "be someone" in this sense could mean dramatically different things depending on the positions idealized in the book or inhabited by actual readers. Richard Brathwaite's *The English Gentleman* (cat. 44), for example, aimed to fashion a genteel English identity. The categories displayed on the frontispiece track idealized stages in a man's life, while also identifying the social spheres in which success could be imagined or cultivated (*Edvcation, Vocation, Recreation, Acqvaintance*). The final category, *Perfection*, has a Latin tag ("Heaven is sought on this road") that posits a further and final ideal, the divine point at which social practices will find their ultimate use and meaning. This non-social and non-temporal point to which the book conducts its readers adds an additional ideological layer to the book's construction of Englishness.

John Bulwer's *Anthropometamorphosis* (cat. 45) is essentially a how-*not*-to book, guiding the reader toward an unadulterated Englishness by cataloging, as antitypes, practices involving the manipulation of the body (including tattooing, piercing, tongue-splitting, neck-stretching and earlobe elongation). The English body that implicitly emerges as normative (because "natural" and untouched) is equally invented as an ethnographic body.

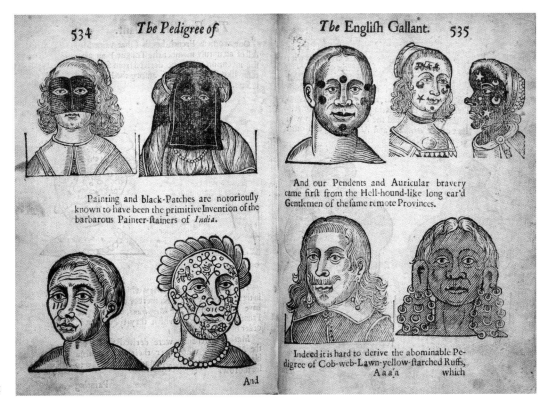

45

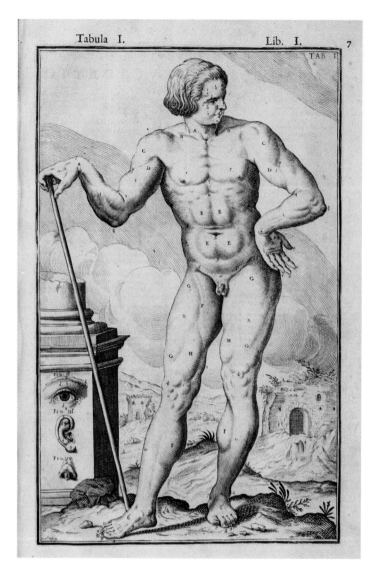

46

46 Giulio Cesare Casserio
(ca. 1552–1616)
Tabulae anatomicae LXXVIII
[Amsterdam: apud Iohannem
Blaev, 1645]. Forms part of:
Adriaan van de Spiegel
(1578–1625). *Opera quae extant,
omnia.* Amsterdam: apud Iohannem
Blaev, 1645
John Crerar Collection of
Rare Books in the History of
Science and Medicine

Giulio Cesare Casserio's engraving of the human form, as printed in Adriaan van de Spiegel's anatomy (cat. 46) may look like a natural body. And yet, like the bodies in Brathwaite's and Bulwer's texts, it emerges within a specific discourse with its own orders of representation. Understood this way, the anatomical atlas is also an ideologically charged how-to book, not only for students of anatomy but also for all those learning to imagine and inhabit their own bodies as the objects and subjects of scientific knowledge.

47 Nicholas Culpeper
(1616–1654)
The English Physitian:
Or An Astrologo-Physical Discourse
of the Vulgar Herbs of this Nation
London: by Peter Cole, 1652
John Crerar Collection of
Rare Books in the History of
Science and Medicine

Designed to help readers "look after" themselves, self-help books necessitated a process of self-reflection, of moving beyond the self in order to look back at it. If conduct books exposed the outward and theatrical dimensions of person-hood, self-help books looked inwards to physiology and psychology, often highlighting the psychological and emotional impact of socialization.

Nicholas Culpeper's herbal (cat. 47), a compendium of natural cures, gives its reader tools for self-diagnosis and self-healing. The reader of this book looked toward a future self and also measured his or her present self against an implied norm, such that anger, sorrow or melancholy, for example, could be understood as conditions to cure. While books like this allowed readers to be their own physicians, they also subjected them to norms of health that potentially marked everyday emotions and reactions as symptoms of pathology.

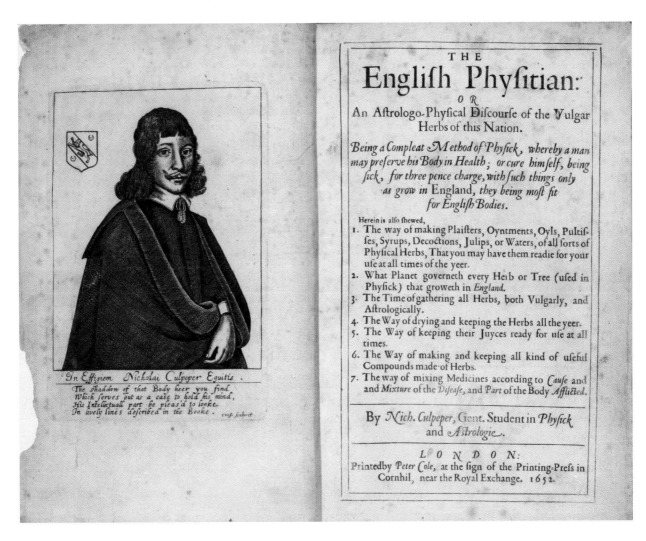

47

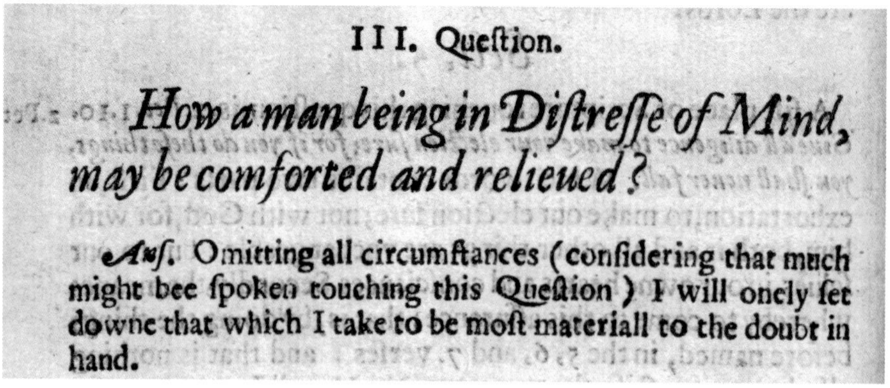

III. Question.

How a man being in Diſtreſſe of Mind, may be comforted and relieued?

Anſ. Omitting all circumſtances (conſidering that much might bee ſpoken touching this Queſtion) I will onely ſet downe that which I take to be moſt materiall to the doubt in hand.

48

48 William Perkins
(1558–1602)
The Whole Treatise Of The Cases Of Conscience
London: by Iohn Legatt, 1628
Rare Book Collection

49 Robert Burton
(1577–1640)
The Anatomy Of Melancholy
Oxford: by Iohn Lichfield and Iames Short, for Henry Cripps, 1621
Helen and Ruth Regenstein Collection of Rare Books
Not illustrated

Like Culpeper's medical book, William Perkins's religious treatise on "case conscience" (cat. 48) offers itself as a vehicle for psychological self-analysis and self-cure, even as it prescribes conventional moral conduct. Doing for the soul what Culpeper does for the body, Perkins teaches how to guard against despair by looking inward to examine conscience, but also how to prevent self-delusion by looking after conscience and developing it through a continual process of self-reflection.

Throughout his life, the Oxford scholar and librarian Robert Burton added to and revised his 1621 *Anatomy of Melancholy* (cat. 49, not illustrated), a massive compendium on the social and psychic conditions of melancholia. In the process of writing to look after himself, Burton created a wildly self-reflexive text, whose obsessions and digressions express precisely the difficulty of grasping something so elusive as melancholy. Burton thus converts the very idea of self-help into an opportunity for theorizing the book itself as cure.

50 Willem Lodewycksz
    (fl. 1598)
    *Premier Livre De L'Histoire De La
    Navigation Avx Indes Orientales,
    Par Les Hollandois*
    Amsterdam: chez Cornille
    Nicolas, 1609
    Rare Book Collection

The how-to books featured here aimed to orient their users as they made their way in the world, geographically, culturally, professionally or socially. Willem Lodewycksz's history of Dutch travel to the East Indies (cat. 50) combines highly practical geographical information (such as representations of specific islands in the archipelago for the use of sailors navigating dangerous straits) with cultural descriptions useful to both real and armchair travelers.

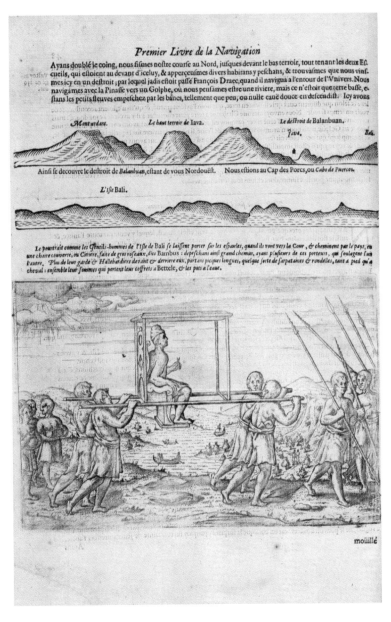

50

51 Thomas Powell
    (1572?–1635?)
    *Tom of All Trade. Or The Plaine
    Path-way To Preferment*
    London: by B. Alsop and T.
    Fawcet, for Benjamen Fisher, 1631
    Rare Book Collection

Making one's way at home also required instruction. An offshoot of the conduct manual, Thomas Powell's early career guide, *Tom of All Trades* (cat. 51), maps out a social and economic terrain for the aspiring class. By cataloging and describing possible occupations and "pathways to preferment," it gives the aspiring outsider an insider's view and a way to imagine social mobility. That said, while the book offers an array of career options, its distinctions also work to reinscribe the occupational hierarchies that could exclude this or that Tom from the preferment promised.

> 34 TOM *of all Trades*,
>
> *A maker of Cordage, Tackle, &c.*
> *A Lymner.*
> *A Clothier, a Clothworker, and a Dyer.*
> *A Taylor, Shooe-maker, Glover, Perfumer,
>   and Trimmer of Gloves.*
> *An Imbroiderer.*
> *A Feltmaker, a Glasier, and one that can
>   paint in Glasse.*
> *Briefly, any Manufacture or trade, wherein
>   is any Science, or Craft.*
> Onely those Trades are of least use and benefit, which are called Huswives Trades (as *Brewer, Baker, Cooke,* and the like.) Because they be the skill of Women as well as of men, and common to both.
> I would have you know, that the Maker was before the Retaylor, and most Shopkeepers are but of a sublimated Trade and retayle, but as Attorneyes to the maker. But if the Maker (without dispute of Freedome in any Corporation, might set up Shop and sell his commoditie immediately) it would be a great deale better for the Commonwealth, than now it is.

51

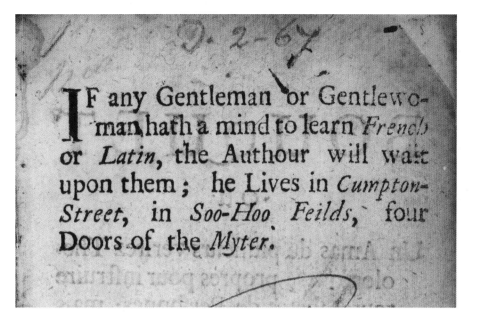

52 Jeremy Taylor
    (1613–1667)
    *The Golden Grove. A Choice
    Manual, Containing What is to be
    Believed, Practised and Desired or
    Prayed for; the Prayers being fitted
    to the several Days of the Week*
    London: for J. M. for
    R. Royston, 1685. 15th ed.
    Rare Book Collection
    Not illustrated

53 Peter Berault
    (fl. 1680–1700)
    *A Nosegay Or Miscellany of several
    Divine Truths, for the Instruction of
    all Persons; but especially for the
    consolation of a troubled Soul*
    London: by T. M. for the
    Author, 1685
    Rare Book Collection

54 Francis Bacon
    (1561–1626)
    *Sylva Sylvarvm: Or A Naturall
    Historie. In Ten Centvries*
    London: by J. H. for
    William Lee, 1628
    John Crerar Collection of
    Rare Books in the History of
    Science and Medicine
    Not illustrated

53

Devotional manuals are designed, of course, to help readers find their ways to the ultimate reward: God. Jeremy Taylor's immensely popular devotional (cat. 52, not illustrated), a late example of the genre, directly connects theological ideals and quotidian practice: by fitting specific prayers "to the seueral Days of the Week," Taylor allows his readers to orient themselves beyond time. Peter (Pierre) Berault's book (cat. 53) moves the reader in the opposite direction. Nominally a devotional, it is also a language manual, printing all of its prayers in English and French on facing pages. Indeed, Berault uses the book's front flyleaf to advertise his skills as a language tutor, and to provide directions to the house where he gave Latin and French lessons. Readers of his book could orient themselves to the divine, in order then to perfect a worldly skill.

In contrast to how-to manuals that offered particular maps for their readers to follow and perfect through their own experience, the practical experiments proposed in Francis Bacon's posthumously published *Sylva Sylvarum* (cat. 54, not illustrated) required readers to explore the *how* of the how-to book. Gathering together a miscellany of observations and experiments for the reader to consider and in some cases perform, the book is a reflection on the instructional manual, a text that illustrates for the reader the empirical process of starting in a "Heape of Particulars" (A1r) and moving toward scientific theory.

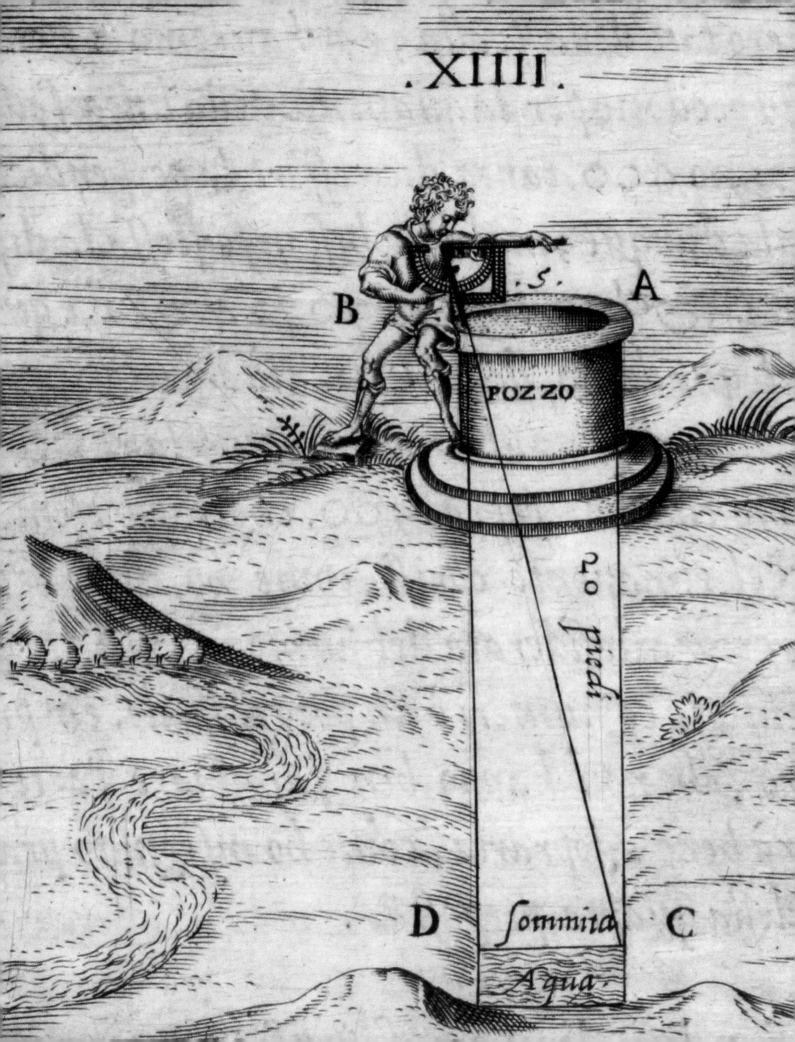

. XIIII .

B

A

S

POZZO

20 piedi

D

Sommita

C

Aqua

PART IV   *Dimensional Thinking*

"DIMENSIONAL THINKING" focuses on books about
the calculation and representation of time and space in fields including
geometry, astronomy, anatomy, art history, theology and criminology.
In particular, it examines how physical forms and features such as
illustrations, pop-ups, foldouts and movable discs (volvelles) helped
the reader to think beyond the two-dimensional space of the page.
Books about measurement by nature evoke a world of reference and
utility outside the book. It is not surprising, then, that many of
them seem to exceed their own material bounds, whether through
foldouts that expand the spatial dimensions of the page or by paper
constructions (pop-ups) that convert the page from a two- to three-
dimensional object. With such books, use means practice in the most
explicit sense, since their readers are asked to use their hands to
manipulate the matter of the book in order to apprehend it and so
(often literally) unfold knowledge.

Some of these books attempt to give the reader access to things
not usually evident, to secrets and hiding places, to the interior of
the body, to the elusive space of the psyche. Books on the art of
memory are important here, since they aimed to construct and to
expose such places, instructing readers to visualize in spatial terms
both the contents of their memories and the temporality of the
memory process itself.

By enabling readers to move, materially and conceptually, between
different dimensions, all of these books from the mathematical and
human sciences positioned themselves as models for the mind at work.

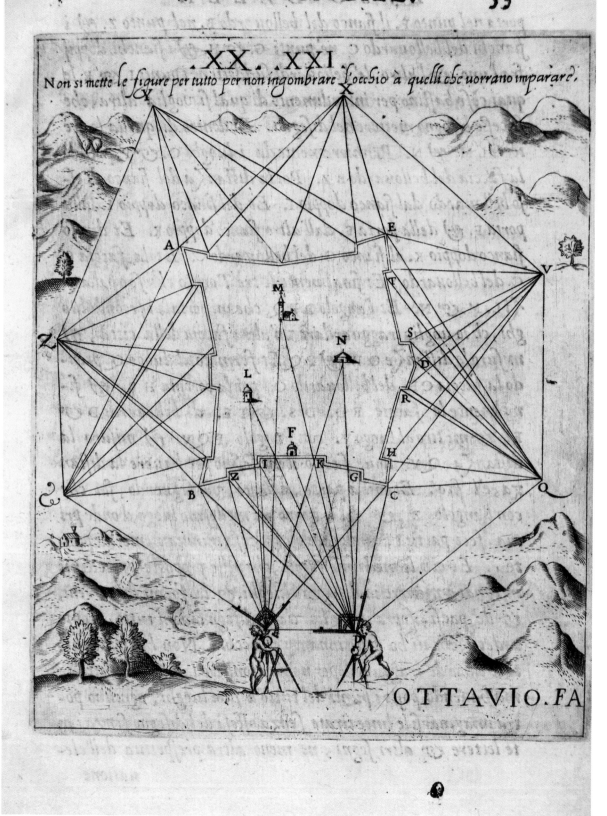

Measuring Space

Geometry (from the Greek for "measurement of the earth") exists at the border between theory and practice. Books on geometry are attentive to the relationship between abstraction and application as that informs their own usefulness and relevance as text. The three treatises in this section present specific instruments of measurement as technologies through which geometry might be practically and theoretically advanced. At the same time, they demonstrate the extent to which the book itself was a technology: in the manner of Dürer's great *Art of Measurement* (cat. 1), all three are in vernacular languages, making them available to a relatively broad range of readers and practitioners, and all combine explanatory narrative and graphic illustration as mutually reinforcing forms of instruction. These are, moreover, small books, easily portable and therefore usable within the actual situations or scenes of measurement that they variously represent.

Ottavio Fabri's beautifully illustrated treatise on the *squadra mobile*, a newly invented adjustable set square (cat. 55), promoted the instrument by demonstrating its theory and usefulness to cartographers, surveyors, navigators and others involved in the measurement of distance and depth. The first part of Leonard Digges's *Geometrical Practise* (cat. 56) similarly teaches Euclidean principles through the application of traditional instruments such as the geometric

56

57 Leonhard Zubler
(1563–1611)
Fabrica et vsvs Instrvmenti
Chorographici: Das ist, Newe
Planimetrische Beschreibung
Basel: in verlegung Ludwig
Königs, 1607
John Crerar Collection of
Rare Books in the History of
Science and Medicine

57

square, semicircle and planisphere. The illustration shown underscores Digges's sense that practice perfects knowledge of theoretical principle. This is a point that Digges makes in terms of his own book: by "searching out the reason and demonstration" of the book's basic principles, he notes, "the diligent practizioner" will learn to think for himself and discover or "inuent manifolde meanes to resolue the like or other stranger questions" (L3v).

The Greek "Pantometria" of Digges's title promises a measurement useful everywhere; implicit here is a kind of utopian ideal of a fully measurable universe, an ideal, notably, that includes some very worldly uses. Like Fabri's manual, Leonhard Zubler's book (cat. 57) was also an advertisement for a new chorographic instrument, usable in a number of contexts for measuring land. The chapter heading to the military illustration shown translates "How to measure the width of a moat and height of a wall to be breached." The picture makes vivid just how important, in an age of military and technological expansion, manuals of measurement were for practicing and perfecting the art of war.

Coordinating Time

Many early astronomy books included within them paper tools for practicing the theoretical knowledge they taught. Peter Apian's *Astronomicum Cæsareum* or "Astronomy of the Caesars" (cat. 58) is one of the most remarkable printed works from the sixteenth century. It includes thirty-six elaborate, hand-colored woodcuts, twenty-one of which included woodcut volvelles, designed to help the reader identify planetary positions and alignments as well as other astronomical phenomena. The volvelle (Latin *volvere*, "to turn") is a revolving disc,

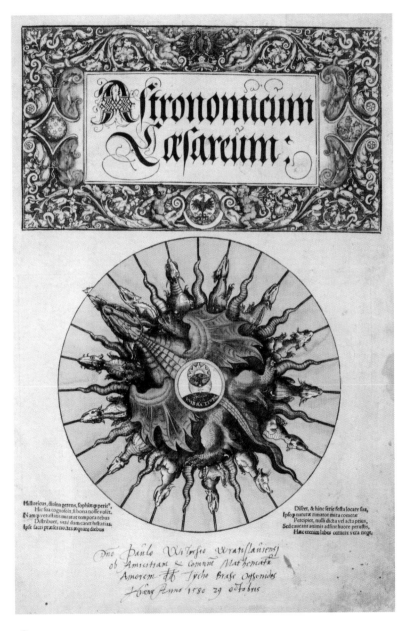

58A

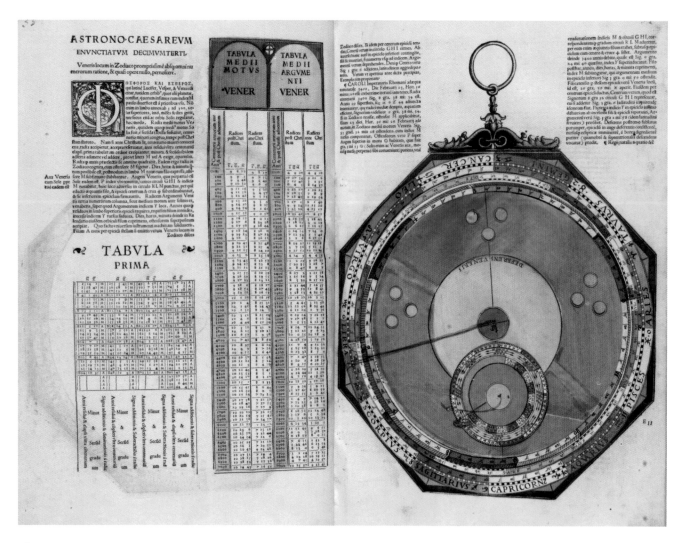

58B

sometimes consisting of multiple layers. On the page shown (58B), there are in total five separate and movable layers. The weighted threads extending from the circles' centers allowed the user to calculate spatial positions and relations for particular times. The book was useful for making scientific calculations of astronomical phenomena within the Ptolomaic system, and also for making astrological calculations for the creation of horoscopes or the identification of propitious and unpropitious times.

Forty years after publication, this copy of Apian's book was given by the great Danish astronomer Tycho Brahe to a student, a gift recorded in Brahe's hand on the title page. By 1580 the diffusion of Copernicus's theories would have diminished the astronomical value of the book to those like Brahe. So the transaction between teacher and student, which must have been prompted by the book's extraordinary aesthetic beauty and monetary value, can also be seen as putting the book to one further use in consolidating this collegial friendship.

Toward Another Dimension

59 Euclid
The Elements Of Geometrie...
With a very fruitfull Praeface made
by M. I. Dee, specifying the chiefe
Mathematicall Sciences
London: by Iohn Daye, 1570
Rare Book Collection,
Joseph Halle Schaffner Bequest

Geometry tracks the shift from one dimension to another: point to line, line to square, and square to cube. In the move to solid three-dimensional bodies, the page reaches a material limit. All three books illustrated here deploy textual strategies to aid the imagination at that limit. In the first English translation of Euclid (cat. 59), the eleventh book (on solids) came equipped with a series of paper inserts for the reader to affix to given diagrams, thereby supplementing the page in order literally to project it into a third dimension.

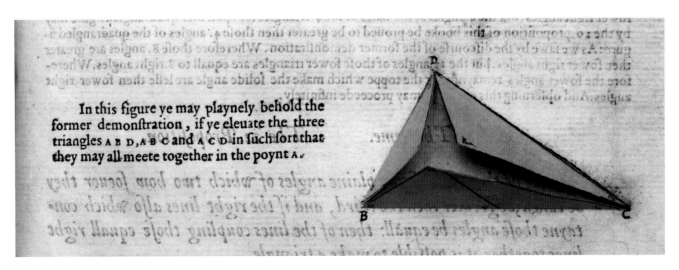

59

60 Vincenzo Coronelli
(1650–1718)
Epitome Cosmografica
Cologne: Ad istanza di Andrea
Poletti in Venetia, 1693
Rare Book Collection,
Gift of John Fleming

Vincenzo Coronelli's cosmographic atlas (cat. 60) came equipped with far more elaborate and geometrically detailed foldouts. These extend the space of the page and the book, transforming their rectilinear shape into a circle in order to represent the terrestrial and celestial globes. The foldouts allow readers to use the text as a substitute for the scientific instrument (the telescope) that produced them. That said, it is notable how fragile the manipulable pages are as tools, and what a delicate touch is required to unfold them and return them back to the space of the book. Might it be that copies of Coronelli's book in which these maps are so well preserved are those that were, in fact, never used?

60A

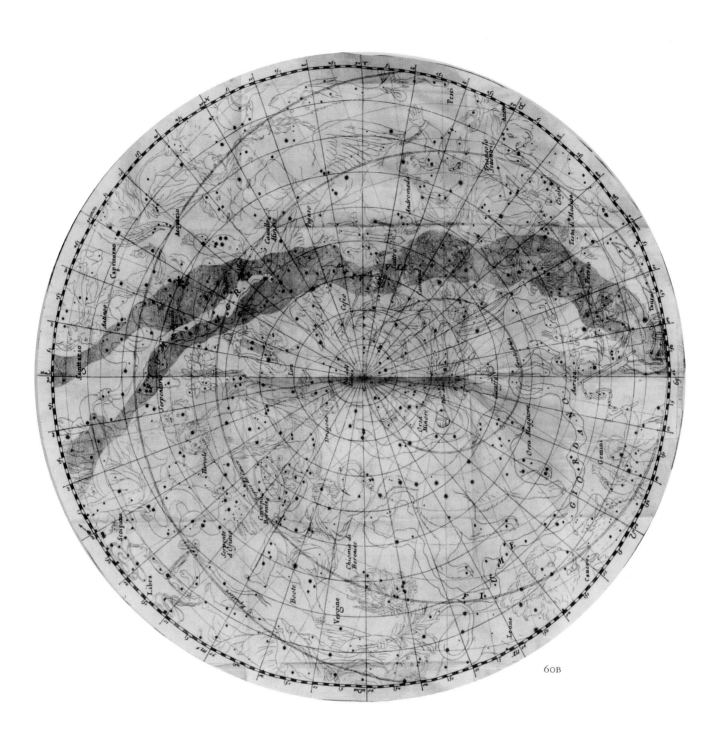

60B

61

61 Humphrey Prideaux (1648–1724)
Marmora Oxoniensia
Oxford: E Theatro
Sheldoniano, 1676
Rare Book Collection,
Berlin Collection

In contrast to extendable paper surfaces, the arts of perspective and chiaroscuro offered ways of representing depth or three-dimensionality using only the flat plane of the page. The engravings in Humphrey Prideaux's guide to the Earl of Arundel's collection of classical marbles (cat. 61) depict statues and reliefs through the use of light and shadow (chiaroscuro). The figures seem to emerge from the page, but less as natural human bodies than as distinctly sculptural forms, suggesting the priority of aesthetic mediation in these portrayals of the human. While engraving technique allowed the page to approximate the contours of space in the material world, it also encouraged a more self-conscious attention to the aesthetics of dimensional representation.

62 Johan Remmelin
    (1583–1632)
    A Survey Of The Microcosme:
    Or, The Anatomy of the Bodies of
    Man and Woman
    London: for Dan. Midwinter, and
    Tho. Leigh, 1702
    John Crerar Collection of
    Rare Books in the History of
    Science and Medicine

To discover is to uncover: the two books featured here help readers see beneath the surface. The interactive, layered illustrations in Johan Remmelin's anatomical atlas (cat. 62) allow the reader to replicate the process of dissection by folding back consecutive bodily surfaces: from skin to muscle and organs; to arteries, veins and nerves; to bone. The flap-book invites its user to "practice" anatomical discovery by moving between the facing pages: between image and index, looking and reading, dividing and ordering. The negotiation between text and image involves the reader in a second movement down into the layers of the book and body. This process of uncovering is at once empirical in orientation and symbolic. It is notable, for example, that the unfolding of the skulls in the images shown (cat. 62A and cat. 62C) transforms a traditionally iconic *memento mori* into physiology, and that the leaves and cloud covering the man's and woman's genitalia invite the reader to find a new kind of scientific knowledge within a symbolics of modesty and immodesty.

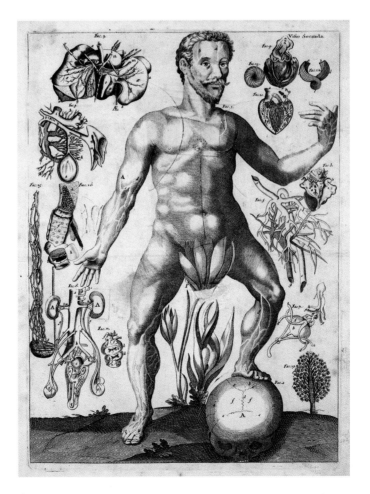

62A

Facio I. in *Vision* III.

FIGURE A. represents.

a. The Frontal vein.
b. The Temporal vein.
A. The head vein.
c. The Liver vein.
d. The *Vena Mediana.*
e. The *Salvatella.*
f. The *Cephalica* of the hand.
g. The *Vena furalis exterior*, or the exterior Vein of the calf of the Leg.
g. The *Suralis interior*, or the inner Vein of the calf of the Leg.
h. The *Ischias major.*
i. The *Saphena*, or Ankle vein.
k. The vein of the great Toe.
l. The *Hypogastrick.*
m. The hair of the Privities.
n. o. p. The *Pudendum.*
q. The *Rima Magna.*
s. The *Clitoris.*
t. The Lips of the *Pudendum.*

The next thirteen Figures are explain'd in *Vision* II. Facio I. and the References are the same.

FIGURE B. The *Peritonæum.*
FIG. C. The Diaphragm.
FIG. D. The Stomach.
FIG. E. The Liver.
FIG. F. The Bladder.
FIG. G. The *Omentum*, or Caul.
FIG. H. The Intestines.
FIG. I. The *Vena Porta.*
FIG. K. The Cavity of the lower Belly.
FIG. L. The Heart.
FIG. M. The *Trachea*, or Wind-Pipe.
FIG. N. The *Aorta*, or great Artery.
FIG. O. The Vertebres of the Breast.
FIG. P. The Womb.
m. m. The Spermatick Blood-vessels.
s. A Branch of the Spermaticks running to the *Peritonæum.*
p. The bottom of the Womb.
q. The Neck, and *Vagina* of the Womb.
r. r. The branches of the Blood-vessels of the lower part of the Womb creeping to its neck.
s. s. Vessels from the Spermatick Arteries to the upper part of the Womb.
v. v. The *Tuba Fallopiana.*
x. x. The *Ovaria*, formerly called the Woman's Testicles.
y. y. The *Ligamenta rotunda* of the Womb.

The other References in this Figure are the same as those in *Vision* II. Facio II. and are there explained.

Facio II. in *Vision* II.

FIGURE A. Represents.

a. b. c. The lower and outer surface of the Skull.
b. The great hole of the *Os Occipitis.*
c. c. The large processes of the *Os Occipitis.*
c. c. The *Processus Styloides* of the temporal Bones.
d. d. The cavity of the temple Bones for the Articulation of the lower Jaw.
e. The prominence of the upper Jaw near the Temples.
f. The *Os Jugale.*
g. d. 4. The *Os Sphænoides*, or wedg like Bone.
h. A. The processes of it called *Processus Pterygoides.*
i. i. The upper Jaw.
k. k. The Teeth of the upper Jaw.

FIGURE B. represents.

a. a. a. The Dura mater.
b. b. b. The blood Vessels dispersed through the Dura Mater.

Facio III. in *Vision* III.

Represents.

a. b. c. d. f. The Cerebellum turned up after the *Medulla oblongata* has been separated from it.
a. The right side of the Cerebellum.
b. The left side of the Cerebellum.
c. The *processus vermiformis.*
e. e. A part of the Cerebellum to which the *Medulla oblongata* is united.
f. That cavity, which with the *Sinus* in the *Medulla oblongata* makes the fourth Ventricle.
g. g. Some part of the Brain adhering to the Cerebellum.

Facio IV. in *Vision* III.

Represents.

a. a. a. The Brain with its ri-

On the other side of this figure.

c. c. The *Pia Mater.*

FIGURE C. represents the Basis of the Brain.

a. a. a. a. The four Lobes of the Brain, *sc.* two anterior, and two hinder.
b. b. The Cerebellum.
c. c. The *Medulla oblongata.*
d. d. The Olfactory Nerves, or first pair.
e. e. The optick Nerves, or second pair.
f. f. The *Nervi oculorum motorii*, or third pair of the Nerves.
g. g. The pathetick Nerves, or fourth pair.
h. h. The fifth pair.
i. i. The sixth pair.
k. k. The auditory Nerves, or seventh pair.
l. l. The *Par vagum*, or eight pair.
m. m. A Nerve from the spinal Marrow called *Nervus recurrens.*
n. n. The ninth pair.
o. o. The tenth pair.
p. p. The trunk of the carotid Artery cut off, where it is divided into the anterior, and the hinder branches.
q. q. The branches which run between the anterior, and the hinder Lobes of the Brain.
r. The anterior branches of the carotid Arteries, which being united, are again divided, and proceed into the fissure of the Brain.
s. The hinder branches of the carotid Arteries united, and meeting with the trunk of the vertebral Artery.
t. t. t. t. The vertebral Arteries, and their three ascending branches.
u. The vertebral branches united into one trunk.
w. w. The place where the vertebral, and carotid Arteries are united, and a branch on each side ascends to the *Plexus Choroïdes.*
x. The *Infundibulum.*
y. y. The two Glands placed behind the *Infundibulum.*
z. z. z. z. The *Pons Varolii*, or the annular protuberance, which proceeding from the Cerebellum embraces the *Medulla oblongata.*

FIGURE D. shews.

a. b. c. D. The internal surface of the upper part of the Skull.
a. a. The cavity of the *Os sincipitis.*
b. The cavity, or concave part of the *Os frontis*, or the forehead Bone.
c. The cavity of the bone of the Occiput.
c. c. c. The thickness of the Skull.

Facio III. in *Vision* III.

Represents.

a. b. c. d. f. The Cerebellum turned up after the *Medulla oblongata* has been separated from it.
a. The right side of the Cerebellum.
b. The left side of the Cerebellum.
c. The *processus vermiformis.*
e. e. A part of the Cerebellum to which the *Medulla oblongata* is united.
f. That cavity, which with the *Sinus* in the *Medulla oblongata* makes the fourth Ventricle.
g. g. Some part of the Brain adhering to the Cerebellum.

Facio V. in *Vision* III.

Represents the inside of the Basis of the Skull, covered with the Dura Mater.

a. The Cavity of the *Os Frontis.*

a. a. a. a. The Dura Mater extended over the Basis of the skull.
b. The *Crista Galli.*
c. c. The Olfactory Nerves.
d. d. The optick Nerves.
e. The *Glandula Pituitaria* with the small end of the *Infundibulum* inserted into it.
f. f. The carotid Arteries com-

---

ings, and *Plica*, or folds.
b. b. The anterior Lobes of the Brain.
c. c. The posterior, and larger Lobes.
c. The Cerebellum.
d. The end of the *Medulla oblongata*, where the *Medulla spinalis* begins.
e. The *Processus mammillaris* of the right side.

And it is to be noted, That because here is a lateral prospect of those parts, we shew only the Nerves of one side, to which there are Nerves answering on the other side.

e. The optick Nerve.
f. One of the *Nervi oculorum Motorii.*
b. One of the pathetick Nerves.
i. One of the Nerves of the fifth pair arising from the *Processus annularis.*
k. l. m. n. The branch of this Nerve distributed to the face and jaws.
k. The branch of this Nerve to the frontal Muscles.
l. The branch assign'd to the Nostrils.
m. The branch, which the temporal Muscle receives.
n. The branch, which goes to the Muscles of the Nose, to the upper lip, and to the roots of the Teeth in the upper Jaw.
p. The branch of this Nerve, which goes to the Palate and Gums.
o. q. r. The second great branch of the Nerves of the fifth pair.
q. The branch which goes to the Parotid gland on the right side.
r. The branch, which is bestowed upon the Tongue.
s. A branch of the fifth pair bestowed upon the lower lip, the teeth of the lower jaw, and the chin.
u. † One of the Nerves of the sixth pair.
f. The branch of it, which goes to some of the Muscles of the Eye.
† The division of this Nerve, which united with some branches of the fifth pair, makes the beginning of the intercostal Nerve.
w. 1. 2. 3. One of the Nerves of the *Par auditorium*, or seventh pair.
1. The branch which goes to the Muscles of the Eye-brows and forehead.
2. u. The Branch which serves for hearing.
3. The branch which is bestowed upon the Muscles of the Tongue, and of the *Os Hyoides.*
x. y. The Nerves of the *Par vagum* on the right side.
x. The beginning of the intercostal Nerve.
z. The *Nervus accessorius spinalis*, which goes to the Muscles of the Neck, and to the shoulders.
4. One of the Nerves of the Ninth pair.
5. One of the Nerves of the Tenth pair.

Facio V. in *Vision* III.

Represents the inside of the Basis of the Skull, covered with the Dura Mater.

a. The Cavity of the *Os Frontis.*

a. a. a. a. The Dura Mater extended over the Basis of the skull.
b. The *Crista Galli.*
c. c. The Olfactory Nerves.
d. d. The optick Nerves.
e. The *Glandula Pituitaria* with the small end of the *Infundibulum* inserted into it.
f. f. The carotid Arteries com-

---

ing out just by the sides of it.
g. g. The *Nervi oculorum motorii* passing through the *Cranium.*
b. b. The pathetick Nerves, which pass out of the Skull at the same hole as the former.
i. i. The Nerves of the fifth pair.
k. k. The sixth pair, which running under the Dura Mater, pass out at the same hole as the Nerves of the third and fourth Pair do.
l. l. The Auditory Nerves.
m. m. The *Par vagum.*
n. n. The recurrent Nerve.
o. o. The Ninth pair.
p. p. The Tenth pair.
q. q. The lateral Sinuses.

Facio VI. in *Vision* III.

Represents the Nerves, which proceed from the third, fourth, fifth and sixth Pairs, and serve to the Muscles of the Eyes, &c.

a. A Nerve from the third pair to the *Musculus attollens*, the *Deprimens*, and the *Adducens* of the Eye, and to one of the oblique Muscles.
b. A Nerve from the fourth pair to the *Musculus Trochlearis.*
c. A Nerve from the sixth pair to the Abducent Muscle of the Eye.
d. One of the Nerves of the fifth pair.
e. A Nerve from the fifth pair, which runs towards the Eye, which is divided into.
f. The upper branch, which serves to the Eye-lids, &c.
g. The lower branch, which serves likewise to the Eye-lids, &c.
h. A Nerve from the third pair, to the Muscle which pulls up the Eye.
k. A branch from the same pair to the Muscle, which pulls the Eye towards the Nose.
l. A branch of the same Nerve to the Muscle, which draws the Eye downwards.
m. A branch of the same Nerve to the *Musculus obliquus minor.*
n. Some small Nerves from the Plexus of the third pair, which pass through the *Tunica Sclerotica* of the Eye, to the *Uvea.*
o. A Nerve from the sixth pair to the Muscle, which pulls the Eye outward.
p. A Nerve from the upper branch, *f.* to the Nostrils.
q. A Nerve from the same branch to the Forehead.
r. That part of the fifth pair, which goes to the lower Jaw, cut off.
s. That branch of the fifth pair cut off, which goes to the palate.
t. A branch of the fifth pair to the Cheeks, to the roots of the upper teeth, &c.

Facio VII. in *Vision* III.

Shews the Ramifications of the Nerves of the fifth and sixth Pairs.

a. The Nerve of the sixth pair.
b. The trunk of one of the Nerves of the fifth pair.
c. Two Twigs which are reflected to make the beginning of the intercostal Nerve.
A A twig to the Nostrils.
e. A twig to the Muscles of the Forehead.
f. f. Two twigs which serve to the Eyelids, and interior gland of the Eye.
g. A branch of the fifth pair to the Eyelid, and exterior glands.
h. A twig to the Muscle called *Masseter.*

---

i. A twig to the Muscles of the Nose.
k. k. k. Several twigs of the fifth pair to the upper Lip.
l. A branch of the fifth pair to the Gums.
m. A branch to the Palate.
n. A Nerve from the fifth pair to the Parotid Glands.
o. A twig to the internal Masticatory.
p. A twig to the external Masticatory.
q. Another twig to the internal part of the same Masticatory.
r. A twig to the root of the Tongue.
s. s. A branch to the substance of the Tongue.
t. A branch of this fifth pair to the parts under the Tongue.
u. u. Some twigs to the lower Lip.
x. x. Some twigs to the chin.

Facio VIII. in *Vision* III.

Shews the Heart opened at the right Ventricle, and the Vena Cava.

a. The right Auricle open'd.
b. c. d. e. The *Vena Cava* open'd.
c. A protuberance in the *Vena Cava*, which turns the course of the Blood towards the right auricle.
d. The place where the *Foramen Ovale* is in a Fœtus.
e. The Orifice of the Coronary Vein.
g. The *Valvula tricuspides.*
i. i. Certain Caruncles called *Papilla Carnea*, to the top of which are joined *k. k.* The Fibrills of the *Valvula tricuspides.*
l. The Cone of the Heart.

Facio IX. in *Vision* III.

Represents the Muscles of the Tongue.

a. a. The *Musculi Styloglossi.*
b. b. The *Musculi Ceratoglossi.*
c. c. The *Genioglossi.*
d. d. The *Musculi Styloglossi.*
e. e. The *Musculi Basioglossi.*
f. The Tongue.

Facio X. in *Vision* III.

Shews the Muscles of the Pharinx.

a. a. The *Musculi Stylopharyngæi.*
b. b. The *Musculi Sphænopharyngæi.*
c. c. The *Cephalopharyngæi.*
d. The *Musculus Oesophagæus.*
e. A part of the *Oesophagus.*
f. The exterior Coat of the *Oesophagus.*
g. The exterior Fibres of the second Coat.
h. The interior Fibres of the second Coat.

Facio XI. in *Vision* III.

Represents the Stomach.

And FIGURE A. shews that part of the Stomach, which lies toward the Back.

a. The Pharynx, or upper part of the Oesophagus.
b. The Tonsills, or Glands on the sides of the Throat.
c. The Glandules on the hinder part of the Oesophagus, by the fifth Vertebre of the Thorax.
d. The left, or upper Orifice of the stomach.
e. Nerves from the *Par vagum* to the stomach.
f. The right, or lower Orifice of the stomach called *Pylorus.*
g. The Duodenum.
h. The Passage of the Gall into the Duodenum.

Facio XII. in *Vision* III.

Shews the interior Superfice of the Muscular Coat of the Stomach.

a. a. a. The Oesophagus.
b. The mouth of the stomach.
c. c. The circular Fibres which contract, and close the mouth of the stomach.
d. *d. d.* A parcel of Fibres, which run along the top of the stomach from the mouth of it, to the Pylorus.
e. The Pylorus.
f. f. f. Other fleshy fibres, which running obliquely from the left-side to the right, go to the bottom of the stomach.

Facio XIII. in *Vision* III.

Represents.

a. The stomach out of place.
b. b. b. b. The Pancreas.
c. c. c. The *Ductus Pancreaticus*, with its Ramifications in the Pancreas.
d. d. The Duodenum.
e. The opening of the *Ductus Pancreaticus* into the Duodenum.
f. f. f. The Jejunum.
g. g. The Mesentery growing to the Jejunum.
h. The large gland of the Mesentery called *Pancreas Aselli.*
i. i. i. Smaller glands of the Mesentery.
k. k. k. The lacteal Vessels in the Mesentery.
l. l. l. The beginning of the lacteal Ducts running between the Membranes of the Jejunum.
m. m. m. The lacteal Vessels running from the Glands of the Mesentery to the Receptaculum Chyli.
n. n. Lymphatick Vessels running from the Liver to the Receptaculum chyli.
o. The *Receptaculum chyli.*
p. p. p. A part of the *Ductus chyliferus.*
q. The trunk of the mesenterick Artery.
r. r. The Blood-vessels and lacteal Vessels in the Jejunum.
s. The outward Membrane separated, and hanging down.

Facio XIV. in *Vision* III.

Represents one of the Salivatory Ducts under the Tongue.

a. a. The twigs of the Duct freed from the Glandules.
b. b. The greater branches.

---

a. c. d. The whole length of the Oesophagus.
† The opening of the *Ductus Pancreaticus* into the Duodenum.
i. i. i. The Blood-vessels of the Stomach.
b. The bottom of the Stomack.
l. A knot of small Glandules in the Duodenum.
m. m. The outward or nervous Coat of the stomach.

FIGURE B.

shews the Second, or Muscular Coat of the Stomach.

a. The Mouth of the Stomach.
b. b. A portion of the Oesophagus.
c. c. Circular Fibres, which serve for the constriction of the mouth of the Stomach.
d. The Pylorus, with part of the Duodenum.
e. B. e. The circular Fibres of the second Coat of the stomack.

FIGURE C.

Represents the internal Superficies of the Stomack, *i. e.* The Glandulous Coat with its Folds or Corrugations.

Facio XV. in *Vision* III.

Shews.

a. a. The Trunk of the Aorta.
b. b. The Trunk of the *Vena Cava.*
c. c. The Emulgent Veins.
d. d. The Emulgent Arteries.
e. e. The Kidneys.
f. f. f. f. The Ureters.
g. g. The right spermatick Arteries.
h. The right spermatick Vein, springing from the *Vena Cava.*
i. The left spermatick Vein proceeding from the Emulgent Vein.
k. k. The Iliack Arteries.
l. l. The Iliack Veins.
m. m. The inner branches of the Iliack Arteries.
n. n. The external branches of the Iliack Veins.
o. o. The inner branches of the Iliack Veins.
p. p. The outward branches of the Iliack Arteries.
q. q. The Hypogastrick Arteries, going to the Womb and *Vagina.*
r. r. The hypogastrick Veins accompanying the said Arteries.
s. s. The branches of the Hypogastrick Arteries going to the bladder.
t. t. The branches of the Hypogastrick Veins going to the bladder.
u. u. Portions of the Umbilical Arteries.
x. x. The bottom of the womb covered with its common Membrane.
A A portion of the *Intestinum rectum.*
y. y. The round Ligaments of the Womb.
z. z. The Ovaria.
1. 1. The *Tuba Fallopiana*, or *Vasa deferentia*, which carry the Ovum from the Ovaria into the Womb.
2. 2. 2. 2. The Fimbria of the Tube Fallopiana.
† † The *Foramina* of the Tube.
3. The Neck of the Womb divested out of its outer Coat, that the Vessels may be seen.
4. The fore-part of the *Vagina* freed from the Bladder.
5. The Bladder of Urine.
6. 6. The Blood-vessels dispersed through the Bladder.
7. The Sphincter of the Bladder.
8. The Clitoris.
9. 9. The Nympha.
a. a. The Lips of the Pudendum.
e. The Urinary passage.
w. The Orifice of the Vagina.

---

c. The common Duct.
d. The orifice of the Duct.
e. The Papilla, which stands before the orifice.
f. A piece of the membrane of the mouth.

F I N I S.

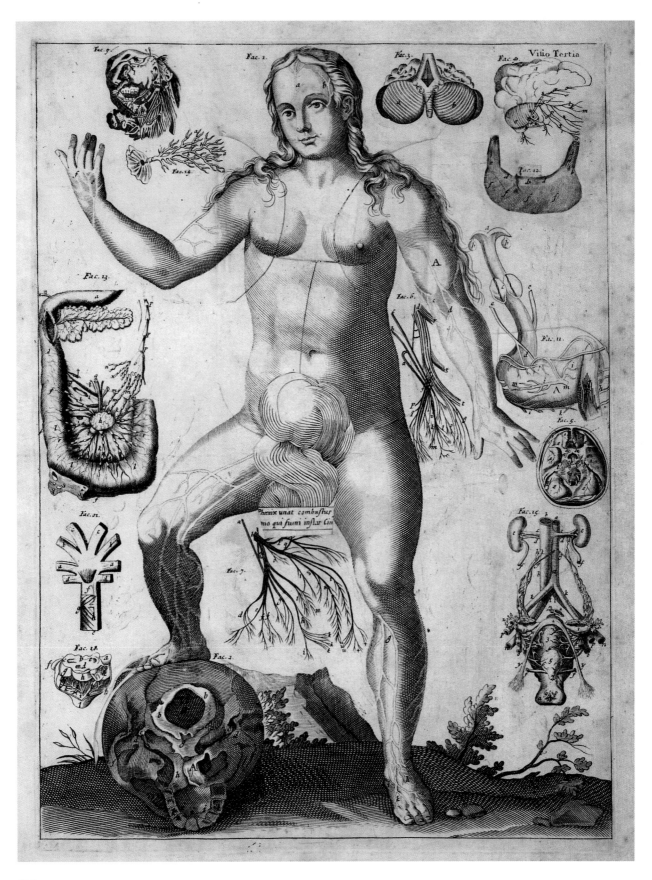

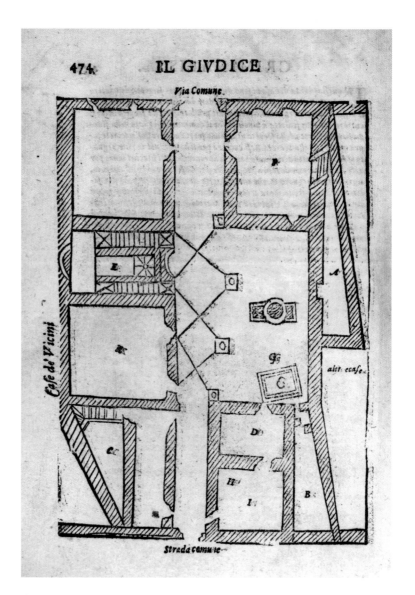

63

63 Antonio Maria Cospi
(fl. 1643)
Il Givdice Criminalista
Florence: Nella Stamperia di
Zanobi Pignoni, 1643
Rare Book Collection,
From the Collection of
Livio Catullo Stecchini

Another early science of discovery is exemplified by Antonio Cospi's *Il Givdice Criminalista* (cat. 63), a manual on criminal investigation with sections, for example, on poison, physiognomy, demonology and forensics. In the illustration shown, included in a section on how to investigate a homicide, Cospi is modeling how a notary might help a judge by drawing a plan of a house so as to expose within it possible secret rooms or hiding places. The accompanying text leads the viewer through the home, detailing entries to the concealed spaces A, B, C, D and E through, for example, a small staircase behind a fireplace in room F, a sinkhole (G) in the central courtyard, a wardrobe (H) in room I, and a spiral staircase descending from the roof at E. In the wrong hands, of course, Cospi's architectural scheme could be used for constructing rather than detecting secret spaces. Useful in practical terms, both Cospi's and Remmelin's books give their readers methods for seeing surfaces less as obstacles to knowledge than as starting points for thought.

Place, Time, Memory

64 Filippo Gesualdo
(d. 1619)
*Plvtosofia. . . Nella quale si spiega
l'Arte della Memoria*
Padua: Appresso
Paulo Megietti, 1592
Rare Book Collection

Acts of memory always require a movement of the mind in time. Memory texts aided memorization by locating or anchoring memory, instead, in space, notably in a familiar room or on the human body. The two illustrations from Filippo Gesualdo's *Plvtosofia* (cat. 64) demonstrate how the art of memory drew on forms of dimensional thinking being perfected in the domains of architecture and anatomy.

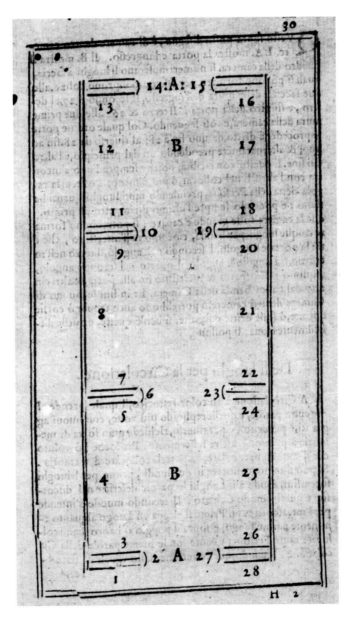

64A

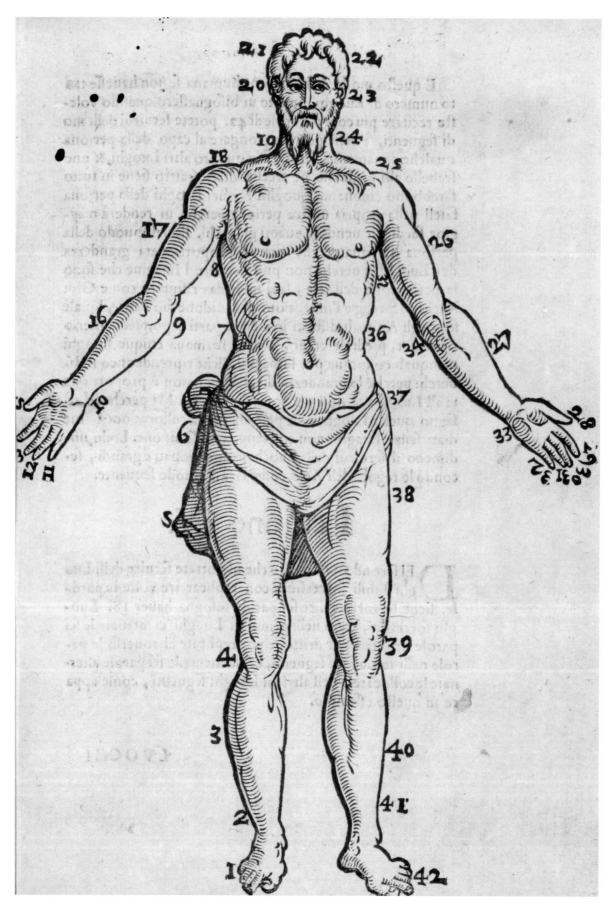

65 Heinrich Döbel
(fl. 1707)
Collegium Mnemonicum
Hamburg: In Verlegung
Samnel Heyll und Johann
Gottfried Liebezeit, 1707
John Crerar Collection of
Rare Books in the History of
Science and Medicine

66 William West
(fl. 1568–1594)
The First Part of Simboleography,
Which May Be Termed the
Art or description, of Instruments
and Presidents
London: by Thomas Wright, 1603
On Loan from a
Private Collection

Heinrich Döbel's memory treatise (cat. 65) depends on the material dimension of language itself, on words occupying both space and time as writing, reading and speaking. As shown in the illustration, Döbel's system for remembering historical dates recodes them as significant letters (as given in Roman capitals) in a simple verbalization of the event to be remembered. As this system reminds us, one of the oldest mnemonic aids is organized language, especially in the form of poetry. The manuscript poem added to the flyleaf of William West's collection of legal forms and formulae (cat. 66) constitutes an art of memory. A popular mnemonic on land conveyance ("Whoe wilbe wise in purchasing"), it lays out a set of simple rules by which a purchaser or attorney could test whether a real estate transaction was secure. In contrast to West's extensive elaboration of prescriptive legal forms, the poem records one reader's attempt to find a simpler and more easily remembered guide to practice.

Museum V. Paries *6.* *XV. & XVI. Sec.* 203

Ve.
Bey der Kunst eines altē Sprachmeisters / da fliegen alle Bienen aus den Bienen-Stöcken in die *noble* Kunst / und machen darinn ein groß GeLauFe.
Tempore Constantini Palæologi, Imp. Orient. Cpolis à Turcis occupatur 1453.

Vo.
Das fährt dem Pabst in seine Ablaß-Briefe / und verbrennt sie bey D. Luthers LeBeN.
Martinus Lutherus contra Indulgentias Papales cœpit disputare 1517.

Vi.
Und lässet dabey gehen ihr Aechzen Himmel-an / unterdessen haben die Münche ihr GeSöF.
Maximilianus I. 1493.

Va,
Hält mit ihrem Gemahl weder Friede noch Treue / sondern liegt stets auf der JaGT.
Fridericus III. 1440.

Ursu.
Und den Kerl im Monde / indem sie durch ihre Finger sahe; fand aber die LuPoS.
Carolus V. 1519.

Museum V. Paries 8. *XVII. & XVIII. Sec.*

Ze.
Für einen / der mit Ruhm genannt
Der dritte Kayser Ferdinand /
Es steht auf dessen Leichenstein:
Hie ruh ich ohne Mühe FeiN.
Ferdinandus III. 1637.

Zo.
Die ihren Freuden-Schmuck angeleget / als der Türcke vor Wien weggeschlagen worden / und im Stich lassen muste das bekante Mutnegra cum MuRVa.
Turcæ Viennensem obsidionē solvunt, in fugam profligati 1683

Zi.
Zur Krönung *Leopoldi*, wobey alle Leute aufsperren die MäuLeR.
Leopoldus 1658.

Za.
Mit dem Kopf vorn hin / ihr Mann / ein Schmidt / schob beyde Beine nach drauf ging er wieder bey den aMBoS.
Ferdinandus II. 1619.

Zu.
Dem Kayser Joseph zum Essen / und sticht sich dabey in eine NaDeL.
Josephus 1705.

Cc 2 BIBLIA

65

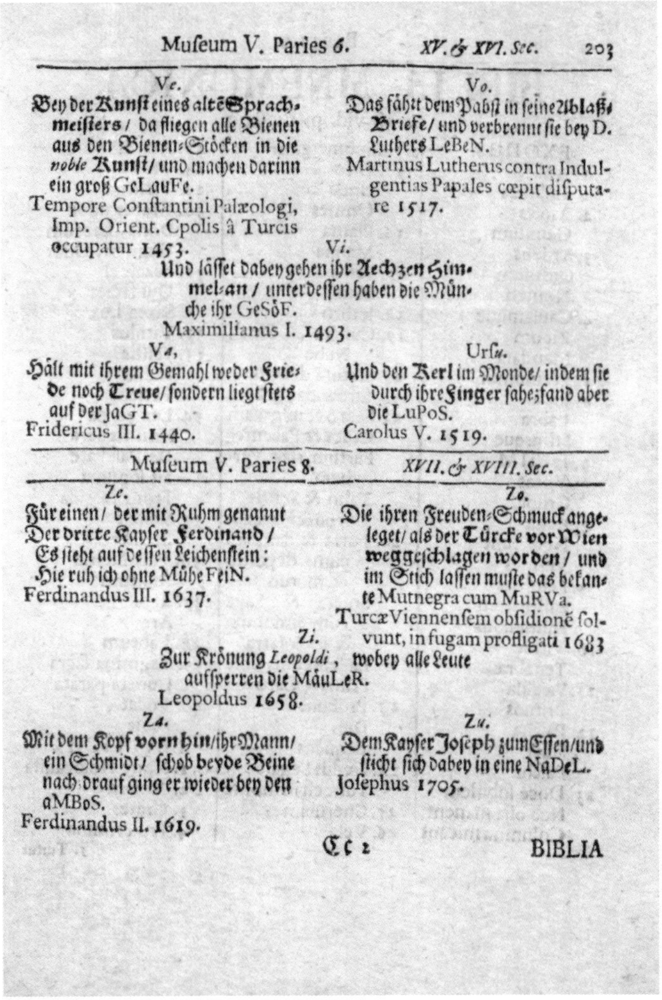

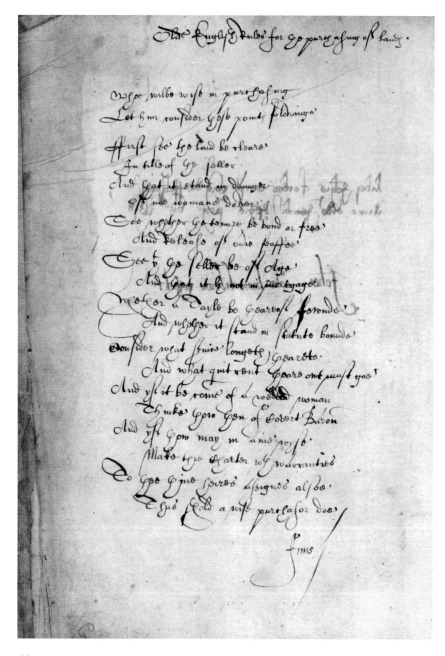

66

Olde English Rules for the purchasing of landes

Whoe wilbe wise in purchasing
Let him consider these pointes folowinge
First see the land be cleare
In title of the seller
And that it stand in daunger
Of noe womans dower
See whether the tenure be bond or free
And Release of eurie feoffee
See that the seller be of Age
And that it ly not in mortgage
Whether a Tayle be theareof fownde
And whether it stand in statute bounde
Consider what seruice longeth theareto
And what quit rent theare out must goe
And yf it be come of a wedded woman
Thinke thow then of Covert Baron
And yf thow may in anie wyse
Make the Charter with warranties
To thee thine heires assignes alsoe
Thus shold a wise purchasor doe.

Finis

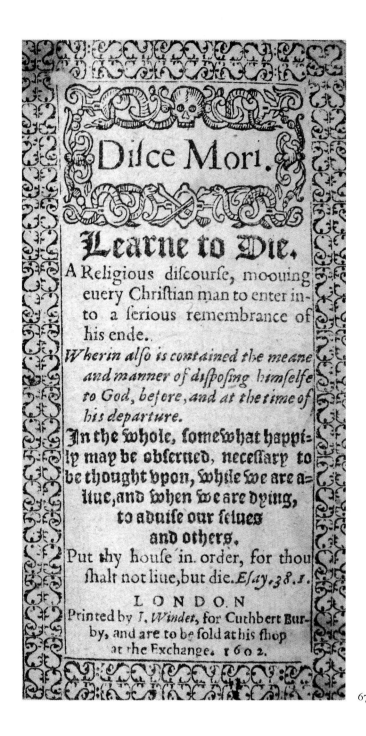

67

67 Christopher Sutton
    (1565?–1629)
    Disce Mori. Learne to Die.
    London: by I. Windet, for
    Cuthbert Burby, 1602
    Rare Book Collection

Christopher Sutton's *Disce Mori* (cat. 67), a collection of devotional meditations on death, undoes the art of memory by calling on the reader, paradoxically, to remember his or her own future, "to enter into a serious remembrance of his ende." In the contexts of the Renaissance arts of memory, the survival of this earlier tradition of the *memento mori* can be seen to constitute a kind of anti-technology of memory, with the sacred dimension of memory trumping the secular.

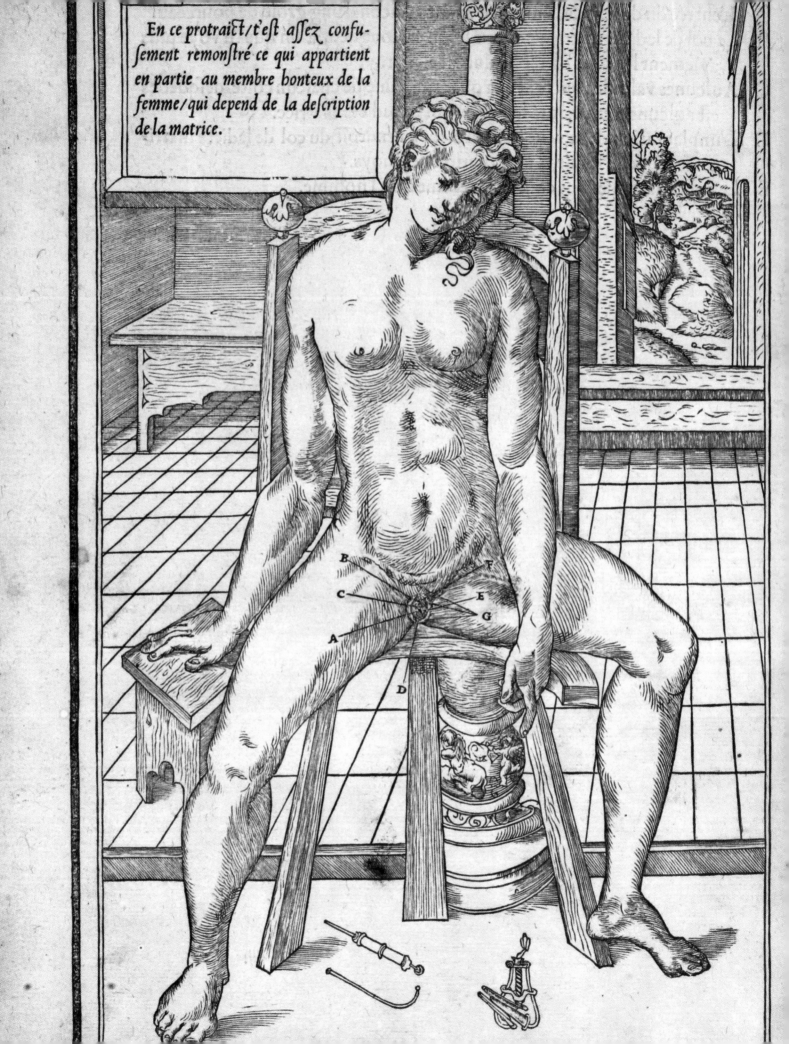

En ce protraict/t'est assez confu-
sement remonstré ce qui appartient
en partie au membre honteux de la
femme/qui depend de la description
de la matrice.

PART V

Taking Liberties

IN CONTRAST TO BOOKS that anticipate and attempt to control their own use, the concern in these final sections is with the unpredictable and often unrepresentable interaction between a book and its reader or a book and its own contents. Drawing on the encyclopedia, on pornography and on books about music, drama and love, "Taking Liberties" explores how books invited or allowed readers to move beyond the printed text: by supplementing their contents, for example, and so challenging their authority; or by misreading them and disregarding norms of use. In addition, it explores how readers were asked to compensate for the liberties that some books took when they represented phenomena beyond the scope of print, more appropriately rendered in other media.

The books featured here have dramatically entered a "relation": with authorities beyond their authority; with readers whose non-conformist use might constitute abuse; and with alternative media that offer different sets of representational possibilities from those of text. All of these relations compromise the autonomy of text. At exactly the same time, they open up a space for the book to emerge as a conspicuously self-reflexive and theorized medium. When the book is confronted with its own limits, in other words, a space for theory becomes possible.

Collective Authority and the Encyclopedia

68 Bartholomaeus, Anglicus
    (13th cent.) and
    Stephen Batman (d. 1584)
    *Batman vppon Bartholome, his
    Booke De Propietatibus Rerum*
    London: by Thomas East, 1582
    Rare Book Collection

An authoritative source for practical and theoretical information, the encyclopedia offers a paradoxically fluid and communal model of knowing, depending for its currency on continual revision, correction and addition. One of the most important such books in early modern England was *Batman vppon Bartholome* (cat. 68), a translation and expansion of an encyclopedia originally written in Latin and compiled by the thirteenth-century English friar Bartholomaeus. Best known now as "Shakespeare's Encyclopedia," *Batman* was an introduction to theological, physiological, medical and natural scientific knowledge. The book's title, like its prefatory list of "contributing authors" both ancient and modern, makes explicit the accretive nature of encyclopedic knowledge. Unsurprisingly, books like this often offered a model for their readers, too, to add to the book, fashioning them as potential participants in the endless project of making and maintaining the encyclopedia.

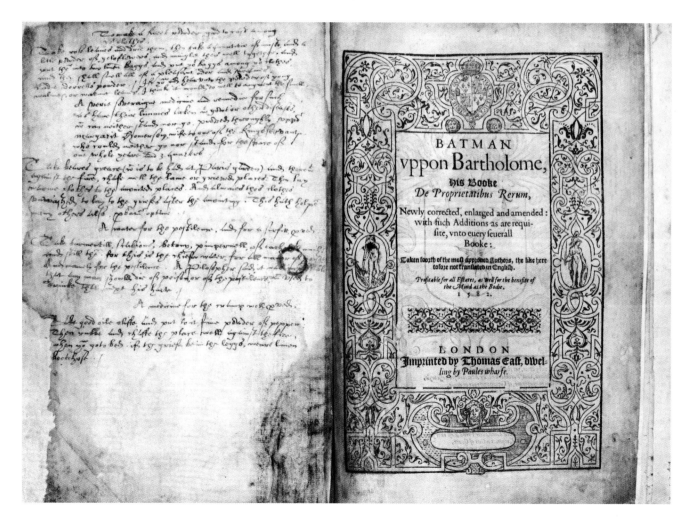

68A

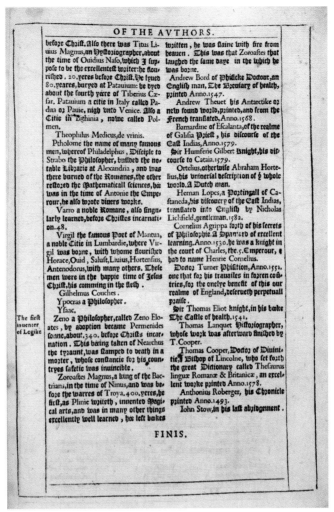

before Christ. Also there was Titus Liuius Magnus, an Hystoriographer, about the time of Ouidius Naso, which I suppose to be the excellentest writer: he flourished, 20. yeres before Christ. He liued 80. yeares, buryed at Patauium: he dyed about the fourth yere of Tiberius Cæsar. Patauium a citie in Italy called Padua or Pauie, nigh vnto Venice. Also a Citie in Bithinia, nowe called Polmen.

Theophilus Medicus, de vrinis.

Ptholome the name of many famous men, whereof Philadelphus, Disciple to Strabo the Philosopher, builded the notable Librarie at Alexandria, and was there burned of the Romanes, the other restored the Mathematicall sciences, he was in the time of Antonie the Emperour, he also wrote diuers workes.

Varro a noble Romane, also singularly learned, before Christes incarnation. 48.

Virgil the famous Poet of Mantua, a noble Citie in Lumbardie, where Virgil was borne, with whome flourished Horace, Ouid, Salust, Liuius, Hortensius, Antenodorus, with many others. These men were in the happie time of Iesus Christ, his comming in the flesh.

Gilhelmus Couches.

Ypocras a Philosopher.

Ysaac.

Zeno a Philosopher, called Zeno Eloates, by adoption became Permenides sonne, about. 340. before Christs incarnation. This being taken of Nearchus the tyraunt, was stamped to death in a morter, whose constancie for his countryes safetie was inuincible.

Zoroastes Magnus, a king of the Bactrians, in the time of Ninus, and was before the warres of Troya. 400. yeres, he first, as Plinie writeth, inuented Magical arts, and was in many other things excellentlp well learned, he left bookes

written, he was slaine with fire from heauen. This was that Zoroastes that laughed the same daye in the which he was borne.

Andrew Bord of Phisicke Doctour, an English man, The Breuiary of health, printed Anno. 1547.

Andrew Theuet his Antarctike or new found world, printed, and from the French translated, Anno. 1568.

Barnardine of Escalanta, of the realme of Galisia Priest, his discourse of the East Indias, Anno. 1579.

Sir Humfrie Gilbert knight, his discourse to Cataia. 1579.

Ortelius, otherwise Abraham Hortelius, his vniuersal description of y whole world. A Dutch man.

Hernan Lopes, a Portingall of Castaneda, his discouery of the East Indias, translated into English by Nicholas Lichfield, gentleman. 1582.

Cornelius Agrippa forth of his secrets of Philosophie. A Spaniard of excellent learning. Anno. 1530. he was a knight in the court of Charles, the. 5. Emperour, had to name Henrie Cornelius.

Doctor Turner Phisition, Anno. 1551. one that for his trauailes in forren countries, for the onelye benefit of this our realme of England, deserueth perpetuall praise.

Sir Thomas Eliot knight, in his booke The Castle of health. 1541.

Thomas Lanquet Hystoriographer, whose work was afterward finished by T. Cooper.

Thomas Cooper, Doctor of Diuinitie, Bishop of Lincolne, who set forth the great Dictionary called Thesaurus linguæ Romanæ & Britanicæ, an excellent worke printed Anno. 1578.

Anthonius Roberger, his Chronicle printed Anno. 1493.

Iohn Stow, in his last abridgement.

FINIS.

68B

This copy of *Batman* is interesting, in fact, for the information added in 1600 and 1605 by one of the book's early readers. Adapting the book to personal needs, the owner used the front flyleaf to record useful practices from other sources, notably local and oral ones. The owner takes care to authorize these as dependable, either by identifying their source or by giving brief testimony regarding the history of their use. In one dramatic instance, a medical remedy is called "soveraigne" because it was used at court, "proved throughly vppon margarit Homerson, wife to one of the Kings servantes."

The owner's additions were not limited to the categories organizing the encyclopedia, nor were they dependent on only traditional or socially sanctioned authorities. One of most striking notes, for example, evokes an authority grounded in local practice and communal experience: "Anno 1600 June 6: The miller of the windmill by Henley vppon Thames shewed me how he preserved his apple trees from the Caterpillers: viz: he vsed everie evening late to shake everie bow of the trees first aboue, then below, and so he did shake many down which lay thick on the grownd. And thereby preserved fruite in aboundaunce. Remember to practice the same."

Use and Abuse: Anatomy and Pornography

69 Charles Estienne
(1504–ca. 1564)
*La dissection des parties du corps
humain divisee en trouis liures*
Paris: chez Simon de Colines, 1546
Rare Book Collection, From the
Collection of Mortimer Frank

Readers are not obliged to use books in the way that an author might like. The three books gathered here, each at the border of anatomy and pornography, blur the bounds between use and abuse. Some of the illustrations in Charles Estienne's medical text (cat. 69) use woodblocks that, in other contexts, had a pornographic function; Estienne adapted these by superimposing on the original image a second plate showing the dissected or anatomized body.

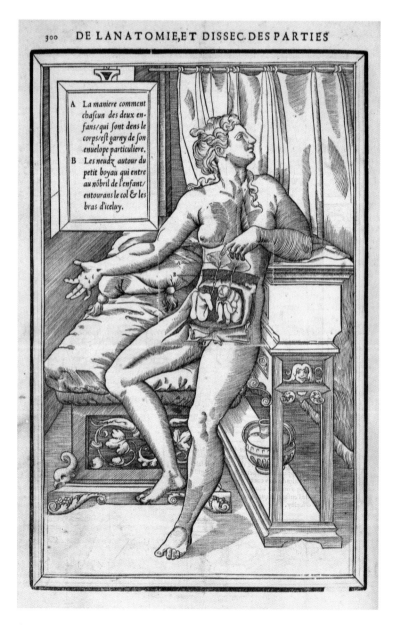

69

70 Helkiah Crooke
(1576–1635)

Mikrokosmographia: A Description of the Body of Man

[London]: by W. Iaggard, 1618

Rare Book Collection, From the Collection of Mortimer Frank

A, B, C. The inner part of the *Peritonæum*.

E E. The embowed part of the Liuer.

F F. The Stomacke.

G, H. That part of the Collicke gut which runneth vnder the stomacke.

I, K. The Membranes by which the wombe adhereth to the bones.

L. The womb ascending as high as to the Nauell.

M, N. Coates arising from the *Peritonæum*, which compasse the Testicles, the vessels and the forepart of the vvombe, and make the outward coate of the same.

O. The fore-part of the necke of the wombe.

P. The place of the bladder.

Q. The *Vrachus*, a Ligament of the bladder.

R R. The vmbilicall arteries.

S. The Nauell.

T. The vmbilicall veyne cutte from the Liuer.

Table x. sheweth the portrature of a woman great with child whose wombe is bared and the Kel taken away, that the stomacke, the guttes and the wombe might bee better seene.   TABVLA. X.

The Vses of the ligaments (like as the *Cremasteres* in men doe suspend the Testicles) to strengthen and corroborate it, as well because of the great burthens it carries often and long, as of the strong throwes in the birth, and the humours which doe flow thither out of the whole body, which doe not onely moysten the part, but also might very well relaxe it. Finally by how much these Ligaments haue more fleshy fibres wouen into them, by so much do they sayth *Pinæus* more leane to the office of muscles, helping the voluntary attraction of mans seede out of the necke into the cauity of the wombe.

The Figure of the wombe.   The figure of the wombe is round [table 8.ᵖ tab. 9.figure 1.ᵃ figure 2.ᶜ] that it might bee the more capacious, and lesse obnoxious to iniuries; aboue, it is somewhat depressed [table 9.figure 3.] like the bladder, excepting the tops of it which they call the hornes. For in woemen with child, as in the bladder so in the womb, the bottome is long and the necke narrow; but in those that be not with childe the bottome is no broader then the necke. *Soranus* and out of him *Falopius* likneth it to a pressed cupping glasse, both for the forme and also for the manner of attraction; for the seed of man cannot attaine vnto the bottome of

70

Conversely, Helkiah Crooke worries in his *Mikrokosmographia* (cat. 70) that a reader might transform his medical text into pornography. In the preface to the fourth book, "Of the Naturall Parts belonging to generation, as well in Men as in Women," he insists that his book has a professional use and is not intended, as some might suppose, to "ensnare men's mindes by sensual demonstrations" (197).

71 Aristotle, pseud.
Aristotle's Master-piece:
Or, The Secrets of Generation
London: [n.p.], 1692
Rare Book Collection,
Gift of Michael Edidin

Crooke's defense of his scientific interests points exactly to the possibility of using texts like this for private pleasure rather than medical or scientific application. The small pseudo-Aristotelian text, *Aristotle's Master-piece* (cat. 71) was a practical guide for midwives, introducing them to female anatomy and to the "secrets of generation." As in the case of Crooke, the author declares in the introduction that he fears lest "*this Book should fall into the Hands of any Obscene or Wanton Person, whose Folly or Malice may turn that into Ridicule, that loudly proclaims the Infinite Wisdom of an Omnipotent Creator*" (A4v). Interestingly, the book was at the center of a later scandal in New England in which the preacher Jonathan Edwards attempted to punish a number of boys for abusing the text by using it to taunt local girls. Unsurprisingly, by warning against misuse, texts like these essentially provided a guide, or at least a spur, to their own abuse.

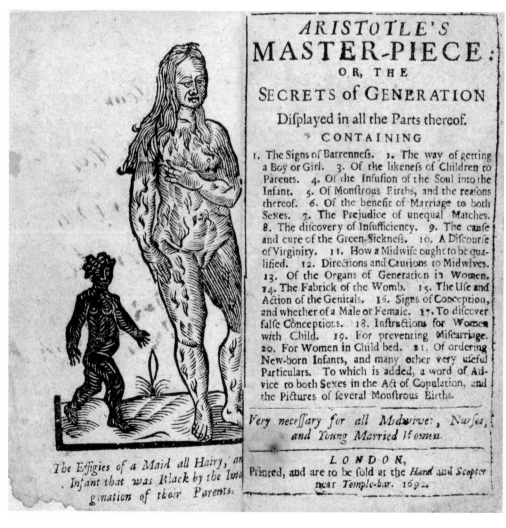

The Effigies of a Maid all Hairy, and an Infant that was Black by the Imagination of their Parents.

ARISTOTLE'S
MASTER-PIECE:
OR, THE
SECRETS of GENERATION
Displayed in all the Parts thereof.
CONTAINING

1. The Signs of Barrenness. 2. The way of getting a Boy or Girl. 3. Of the likeness of Children to Parents. 4. Of the Infusion of the Soul into the Infant. 5. Of Monstrous Births, and the reasons thereof. 6. Of the benefit of Marriage to both Sexes. 7. The Prejudice of unequal Matches. 8. The discovery of Insufficiency. 9. The cause and cure of the Green-Sickness. 10. A Discourse of Virginity. 11. How a Midwife ought to be qualified. 12. Directions and Cautions to Midwives. 13. Of the Organs of Generation in Women. 14. The Fabrick of the Womb. 15. The Use and Action of the Genitals. 16. Signs of Conception, and whether of a Male or Female. 17. To discover false Conceptions. 18. Instructions for Women with Child. 19. For preventing Miscarriage. 20. For Women in Child bed. 21. Of ordering New-born Infants, and many other very useful Particulars. To which is added, a word of Advice to both Sexes in the Act of Copulation, and the Pictures of several Monstrous Births.

Very necessary for all Midwives, Nurses, and Young Married Women.

LONDON,
Printed, and are to be sold at the *Hand and Scepter* near *Temple-bar.* 1692.

71

Beyond the Book: Affect and Medium

Book Use, Book Theory has explored what it means for a book to become useful, and how in that process a book often confronts its own limits as a medium for representing experience or the phenomenal world. Each text in this section is conspicuously inadequate to the task it sets for itself, but through that inadequacy discovers a form of self-reflection, and as such even invents a theory of its own distinctly textual dimensions.

MUSIC AND SOUND

Descartes's treatise on music (cat. 72) opens with a sentence—"The object of this Art is a Sound" (A1r)—that announces both the theorization of his topic and the limitations of the book in respect of its object. The illustration shown here comes from a supplement to the book provided by the English translator.

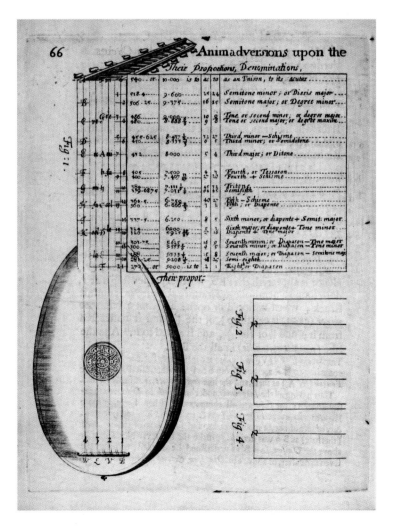

72

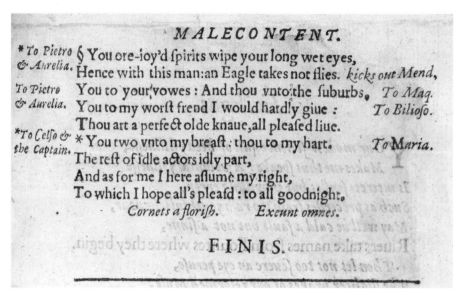

73

73 John Marston
(1575?–1634)
The Malcontent
London: by V.S. for
William Aspley, 1604
Celia and Delia Austrian Study
Collection of Drama 1660–1800

It suggests just how much work needs to be done, in the form of scientific tabulation and division, to approach the acoustical phenomena that are the book's object. It also points, of course, to how Descartes's theoretical explanations of music find their ultimate proof in the practice he himself always had in mind.

PERFORMANCE AND PRESENCE

In the preface to his play *The Malcontent* (cat. 73), John Marston preemptively declares the printed book a failure: "*I would faine leaue the paper; onely one thing afflicts me, to thinke that Scaenes invented, merely to be spoken, should be inforcively published to be read*" (A2r). Marston here confronts the impossibility of a play text's ever fully rendering the presence of the human body in performance. Partly in response to the limitation inherent in using one medium to represent another, the text deploys printed marginalia such as "To Maria" and "kicks out Mend" as stage directions, helpful descriptions of action that render the performative dimension of the play more visible to the reader, in effect making the printed text its own promptbook (see cat. 6).

EMBLEM AND EROS

Because desire is always in search of something not there, it presents a special problem for representation. The two books by Francesco Pona (cat. 74) and Otho van Veen (cat. 75) confront the problem of erotic representation through the use of emblem, a literary form consisting of motto, image, and an explanatory, usually poetic text. Far from being merely decorative, these emblems, one

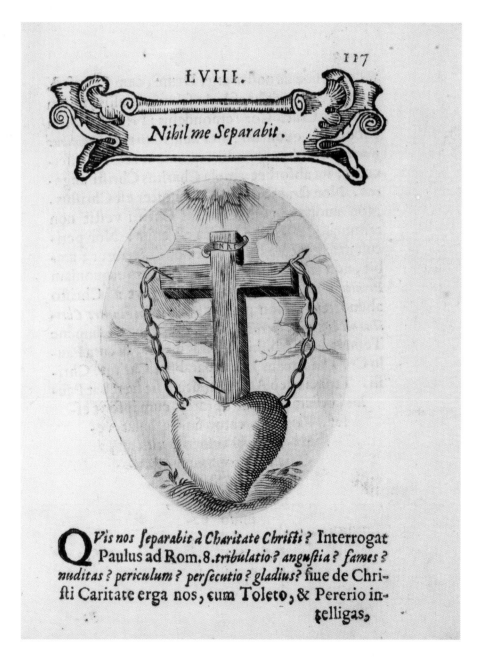

74

secular and one divine, can best be thought of as enabling a difficult kind of cognition, whereby the mind's movement across different and incommensurate media enacts an otherwise unrepresentable dimension of the psyche: the unsettling experience of eros.

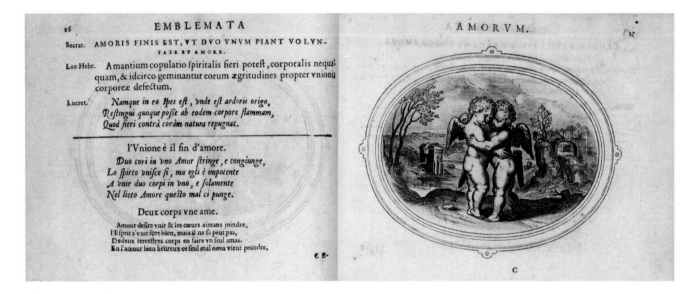